NOR

Corinne Bloch

J·P·M
PUBLICATIONS

Contents

This Way Northern India

Beyond Measure

To anyone with a spirit of adventure, India presents a superb challenge. It never leaves you indifferent. Its magic lies in the sheer profusion of peoples and landscapes enclosed within this diamond-shaped sub-continent, extending over 3,000 km (1,865 miles) from the northern mountains of Kashmir to the southernmost tip of Cape Comorin on the Indian Ocean. East to west, it stretches another 3,000 km from the border with China and Myanmar (Burma) to the Gujarat coast on the Arabian Sea. If superimposed on Europe, it would reach from Sicily to the North Cape.

The bare statistics are enough to make your head spin. By 2010 India—the largest democracy on earth—will have overtaken China as the world's most populous country. People are everywhere, crowding each other into the roadway, bulging out of autorickshaws, perching on roofs of buses and trains, loading a family of four onto a single motor scooter. The ethnic diversity is there to see on a rupee banknote where the sum of money is printed in India's 15 state-recognized languages, in addition to English. Linguists have counted 1,652 languages actually being spoken all over the country (excluding dialects), written in 13 different alphabets. Hindi is spoken by less than a majority of the population, and English by only 3 per cent of the people, mostly in the big cities.

Land of Paradox

Perhaps because of this extraordinary mix of cultures, the modern country soars from one extreme to the other. The cradle of non-violence, it is restless, turbulent, passionate, exhilarating, infuriating. Still 75 per cent rural, India has 300 million destitute people living on its city streets, yet there are no less than 25 million dollar-millionaires, too. While real estate in cities such as Mumbai is the most expensive in the world, the Indian peninsula also harbours Asia's largest shantytowns. Absurdly, in a few years from now, land for construction will be at such a premium that even the tiniest patch belonging to the poorest family will be worth a fortune.

With all the fervour and conviction of days gone by, India still cremates its dead on the banks of the Ganges. Half-naked *sadhu*—ascetics depending entirely on

The windows of Jaipur's Palace of the Winds provided the ladies of the royal harem with a discreet observation post.

charity—pursue their quest for spirituality and redemption, rarely speaking unless reciting their prayers. Meanwhile in Bangalore, Mumbai and New Delhi, young Hindus in jeans and trainers write computer software for American clients and continually reinvent the world of information technology, discussing the terms of their contracts in a polished English that would not be out of place at an Oxford high table.

Anchored in Tradition

Northern India is all the richer in customs and architectural styles because it was more frequently the target of Central Asian and European invaders than the South. After the Aryans, the Persians, the Scythians and the Huns, the Moghuls left the palaces you see when you travel from the green plains of Madhya Pradesh to the Rajasthan desert. Further reminders of this turbulent past are the incongruous Victorian monuments bequeathed by the Raj. Today, the entire Western world, under the guise of progress and modernity, is gradually being assimilated into Indian society.

This capacity to absorb new ideas, whether cultural, economic or religious, without weakening in the slightest their respect for

4

ancestral traditions, has been the greatest strength of the Indian people for more than 3,000 years. As a result, India's culture is one of the most long-lived and fascinating in existence. Neither the influence of the Aryans nor even that of the Muslims has managed to put an end to customs perpetuated since the dawn of time. Indeed, the origins of *ayurveda* medicine, of vegetarianism, of the mother-goddess and the great god Shiva, date back to long before the first invasions and trace their roots to the primitive tribes of the subcontinent.

At the dawn of the 21st century, India's religions still enjoy a healthy following that astonishes the Western world. The country has welcomed industrialization with open arms. It may train 300,000 technicians every year on its university benches, boast the greatest geniuses of information technology and send satellites into space, but nothing seems to dent the power of the Hindu pantheon. It will take more than a few nuclear tests to make Shiva tremble, and more than contact with IBM or Microsoft to westernize Vishnu.

Democratic Revolution
A democracy since the proclamation of Independence in 1947, the nation seems to have successfully adopted a political system that was, at the outset, ill-suited to its diverse population and internal tensions. From one election to the next—and there have been many since the leading parties proved unable to obtain an overall majority—the people are demonstrating more and more their commitment to democratic government.

However, it was not until the 1980s that a proper democratic revolution took place, important enough to transform the political landscape and diminish the historic Congress Party to the advantage of the right-wing Hindu nationalists. Moreover, the steps taken towards economic liberalization in 1991, which swept away the burden of legislative and trade barriers and opened the market to foreign investors, have also favoured the emergence of a new force—200 million consumers. For several years now, the country has revolved around this rising middle class, whose tremendous creative vigour is dismantling the caste system by bringing to the fore people from the lowest levels of society. The arrival of this new class is disrupting the established social order, exacerbating fundamentalism and corrupting the political scene. But eternal Mother India, behind her shimmering veil of traditions, is about to give birth to a new country, more united and stronger than before. 5

Flashback

Early Peoples
India is the cradle of one of our most ancient civilizations, with primitive populations already settled here 50,000 years ago. They lived in small distinct groups sharing forest zones. Considering agriculture to be an insult to the earth, these peoples lived by hunting, and their social structure was based on a matriarchy.

The Dravidians
Later, brown-skinned people with straight black hair, known as Dravidians, appeared alongside these ancient tribes. They possibly represented a branch of a Mediterranean civilization which stretched from Spain to the Ganges before the 3rd millennium BC. Several Dravidian languages, including Tamil, are still spoken in the south of India.

Indus Civilization
From about 2500 BC to 1900 BC, one of the most refined cultures of the ancient world settled in the Indus Basin (present-day Pakistan), spreading over a territory that extended from Rajasthan to the banks of the Ganges. The existence of this so-called "Indus civilization", distantly related to the Sumerians, was revealed at the end of the 19th century, when the ruins of their cities were excavated from a blanket of sand. The modernity of their achievements —streets on a grid pattern, balconied houses, bathrooms, jewellery and a written language— indicates an ancient culture that has reached its zenith. However, there are few clues to help trace its evolution, and its script has still not been deciphered.

Aryan Invasions
It was almost certainly climatic change which drove the pastoral Aryans out of Russia and Central Asia. Whatever the case, these peoples poured into northern India from 1500 BC onwards. Overwhelming the Indus civilization, they imposed new political, religious and social structures of an Indo-European type, similar to those of the Persians and Greeks. Meat-eaters, they are responsible for the present-day difference between the largely vegetarian southern India—which escaped Aryan occupation—and the more carnivorous north.

Religious Evolution
Culturally primitive, these conquerors reduced the Dravidians to slavery but assimilated the more 7

sophisticated Dravidian customs and adopted their gods. The Hindu religion was born of this cultural mix. The first notions of the Hindu god Shiva and the mother-goddess Kali can be traced to the Dravidians, along with the veneration of the cow, while the caste system was imposed by the Aryans, the better to assert their supremacy. The importance of priests—the Brahmans, who represent to this day the highest caste—also owes much to the Dravidians. But it was under the influence of the Aryans that Brahmanism, the archaic form of Hinduism, became a religion characterized by the supreme power of the priests and by the integration of ritual into all aspects of daily life, religious and civil. Buddhism arose in reaction to these constraints in about 500 BC.

Appearance of Sanskrit

The dialects heard today in the north of the peninsula derive from a blend of the language of the Aryan tribes and the tongues of ancient India. This is particularly true of the country's first official language, Hindi. However, for centuries, the sole vehicle of Indian literary culture was Sanskrit, a refined language showing Vedic influence, artificially forged by the Aryans. The sacred texts of Hinduism, the books of the *Veda*, were written in Sanskrit in around 1000 BC. Sanskrit is thus the most ancient of the Indo-European languages of which spoken forms still survive. Greek, Latin, Persian and the Germanic languages all belong to the same linguistic family.

Scythians, Huns and Other Invaders

Whereas the kings of Persia, followed by Alexander the Great, reached the subcontinent but never succeeded in settling there, the Scythians, Iranians and other Aryan tribes in turn occupied the northern regions from 300 BC onwards and founded large empires. The most illustrious of the emperors of the time was Ashoka (c. 269–232 BC) of the Mauryan dynasty, who made the first serious attempt to unify the country. Under his reign, Buddhism rose to be the state religion, and art and culture flourished. (The modern State of India has taken the lion motif of Ashoka's Pillar as its emblem, see p. 69.) In the 4th century AD, the Gupta dynasty succeeded in unifying the North, but the Huns broke up their empire. The remnants were ceded to the Rajputs.

Rajput Clans

The Rajputs controlled the region from the 7th century onwards. They remained part of the political scene first under Muslim domination and later under the British. Their heirs, the maharajahs, even managed to retain their privileges until the middle of the 20th century. No one knows whether their forefathers were Huns or of Indian origin, least of all the Rajputs themselves who blithely created their own mythical genealogy, claiming direct descent from the brother of the god Rama. Being of low birth they were thus able to filter into the warrior caste, the *kshatriya*.

Subsequently, history and legend blended so well, and the Rajputs' chivalrous spirit earned them so much glory, that numerous other dynasties of far more noble lineage falsified their own genealogy to lay claim to Rajput ancestry. Divided into several clans, the great feudal Rajputs shared the region until the 12th century, in an uneasy alliance alternating between brotherhood and bitter internal strife.

Muslim Invasion
At this time, the Arabian peninsula was not unknown to the ancient Hindus, and the city of Makhesvara—Mecca—was one of the sacred places of the cult of Shiva. The birth of the Prophet Muhammad in 570 and the subsequent birth of Islam were destined to overturn the world.

In the 10th century, Muslims settled in Afghanistan. From there they launched their first incursions into northern India, destroying holy places and sacking the city of Varanasi. But it would be another 200 years before Muhammad of Ghur, a Persian prince, took Rajasthan, then Delhi, Varanasi and the whole of the Ganges valley. From then on, the emerging empire never stopped expanding until its fall more than five centuries later.

A slave by the name of Qutb-ud-Din, general and successor of Muhammad, founded the Sultanate of Delhi in 1206; he became the first independent Muslim emperor of India. The "Slave dynasty" reigned until 1290.

Cohabitation with the Hindus
The Muslims never allowed themselves to be absorbed by Hinduism, nor did they succeed in imposing their own religion. Even today, after 800 years, the Islamic/Muslim communities of India and Pakistan represent less than 20 per cent of the total population of the two countries. The dissension which led to the creation of Pakistan, like the conflicts which in India still govern relations between Hindus and Muslims, dates in fact from the days of Qutb-ud-Din.

The large number of Rajput clans made it impossible for the Sultanate to bring all the regions under submission. Relations be-

In the remote villages of Madhya Pradesh, the inhabitants still lead a medieval way of life.

tween the two communities were thus marred by incessant confrontations, but there were also some necessary attempts at collaboration, as witnessed by the emergence at this time of a common language, Urdu. A combination of Persian vocabulary and Hindu grammar, it remains the everyday language of Pakistan and is still spoken in northern India.

Moghul Era

Babar or Babur, descendant of Tamerlane (Timur) and of the Mongol leader Ghengis Khan, reigned over a small sultanate in Central Asia. In 1527, he over-

threw the Sultanate of Delhi and founded the Moghul Empire on its ruins. (The word *Moghul* is the Persian translation of Mongol.) "Hindustan," he wrote, "is a country which reveals very few attractive facets. The inhabitants (…) are without intelligence and coarse (…). They build without concern for beauty or elegance." Babar was destined to have a great influence on Indian architecture, and during the Moghul era monuments as magnificent as the Taj Mahal were built.

Babar was succeeded by his son Humayun, but the empire's most fascinating personality is without doubt his grandson, the

Emperor Akbar, who reigned from 1556 until 1605. Under his rule, all religions were tolerated and he even invented his own, which died with him. He abolished the taxes imposed on non-Muslims and, following a policy begun by his predecessors to consolidate the empire, initiated a process of conciliation towards the Rajputs by naming them heads of his armies and by marrying several Rajput princesses. Indeed, certain Rajasthani families owe to Akbar the prestige which they still enjoy today.

Akbar's successors were not all as enlightened nor as tolerant. Fresh conflicts with the Rajputs, Persian incursions and the rise of the Marathas (a confederation of small Hindu kingdoms in central India) caused the disintegration of the empire—given the final blow by the British in 1803.

Europeans Enter the Scene
Portuguese navigator Vasco da Gama was probably the first European to visit the Malabar Coast in the southwest, arriving in 1498. The Portuguese were also the last to leave India, not relinquishing their colony of Goa until 1961.

The English East India Company only appeared on the scene after the French and the Dutch. Keen to obtain supplies of spices, indigo and silks, it opened a first trading post at Surat at the beginning of the 17th century, with the consent of the Moghuls. The company quickly expanded to establish further posts in Madras, Calcutta and Bombay.

Anglo-French Conflict
During the 18th century, things began to warm up as the colonial ambitions of the British started to overtake their commercial objectives. The control of trade with India became the prize during a century of conflict with the French, a situation which was to have its repercussions on the conflicts between local empires. The British played the Rajputs off against the Marathas, the latter being supported by France.

In 1803, the British captured Delhi from the Marathas. They brought to trial the last Moghul, whose fief had been reduced to the Red Fort, and deported him to Burma. From then on, all of India gradually fell into British hands. Only Nepal, in exchange for a few provinces, would never be incorporated into the British Indian Empire.

Indian Mutiny
India remained an aggregate of states, many of which enjoyed only the appearance of independence. In reality, the new masters imposed their administration on the small states, putting forward

the poor management of business as their reason. Despoiled by the great landowners, thousands of families were reduced to a state of poverty. By virtue of treaties signed with the British, even the Rajput princes became totally subdued. However, they were not deprived of all authority, for the British wanted to ensure their support in case of insurrection—something which did eventually happen in 1857.

The affair which shook the country demonstrates the British lack of sensitivity for the local culture. The sepoys, Indian soldiers in the service of the Crown, were instructed to bite off the tip of their cartridges before inserting them into the rifle breech. But the British had lubricated the cartridges with animal fat which the Hindus were convinced was cow grease and the Muslims thought was pig lard. The furious sepoys triggered off a mutiny which was to spread all over northern India.

Imperial Years

The rebellion, put down with the help of the Rajput princes, only served to reinforce British domination. Henceforth, the British no longer mixed with the Indians, but opened their own clubs and their own schools. They dismantled the palace apartments of the Red Fort to build army barracks, repressed the Hindu culture, abolished certain local customs and promoted English as the national language. However, they gave their assurance that neither race nor religion would prevent Indians from holding government appointments. The British Crown took over the power hitherto wielded by the East India Company, and in Delhi Queen Victoria was proclaimed Empress of India on January 1, 1877.

Path to Independence

On the British side, a liberal thread began to appear in literature and politics. Indians were authorized to hold key positions and saw part of executive power returned to them. The national Indian Congress movement, founded in 1880, made independence its battle cry. At the beginning of the 20th century, young Indians who had studied in England, such as Mohandas Gandhi and Jawaharlal Nehru, came back imbued with notions of democracy and patriotism.

A dark cloud gathered over the horizon of the Empire. Gandhi organized his acts of civil disobedience and long marches: during the march of 1930, he led an immense following to the sea shore to collect the salt which the British had claimed as their monopoly. The Mahatma's policy of passive resistance and Nehru's determination earned the two new Congress leaders several stays in prison, but also the support of the peasant masses. The world wars further tarnished the Europeans' image in the region, strengthening the nationalism of Indians who left to fight in Europe under the Union Jack.

Independence and Partition
As independence began to appear inevitable, so did a whole series of problems. The new India, for example, would have a Hindu majority, a situation that the Muslim minority considered intolerable. For many years, the leader of the Muslims, Muhammad Ali Jinnah, had been calling for the division of the Empire into two distinct countries, India and Pakistan. Lord Mountbatten, dispatched to Delhi at the beginning of 1947 to settle the question, failed to make him change his mind. Already in 1946 an outbreak of civil war had resulted in 10,000 deaths of both Hindus and Muslims in Calcutta.

The proclamation of Indian Independence in August 1947 provoked an exodus of 10 million people. The new frontiers fuelled religious hatred: whole families of Muslims were murdered trying to reach Pakistan, while hundreds of thousands of Sikhs and Hindus suffered the same fate while trying to emigrate in the opposite direction.

In contrast to the Rajput States, which accepted entry into the Indian Union, Kashmir—with a large Muslim population but governed by Hindus—could not make a decision. Ever since, this territory has been the subject of clashes between the Indian and Pakistani armies.

Independent India
Ghandi, the figurehead of Independence, was not supported by everyone. Even today, Hindu groups reproach him for having assumed the appearance of an ascetic to hide his Anglo-Saxon idealism. Similarly, Congress is accused of sacrificing India's politico-cultural tradition to British ideology, the institution of democracy having resulted in the violent partition of the country, the elimination of the social system and the reduction of the artisan classes to an impoverished proletariat.

In 1948, Gandhi was assassinated by a Hindu extremist for having backed persecuted Muslims. Ali Jinnah, the Governor General of Pakistan, died the same year. His country was split into two opposing regions 2,000 km (1,200 miles) apart, with a hostile India between them. It was not until 1971 that Eastern Pakistan proclaimed its independence and became Bangladesh. Because the region's industries 13 remained on Indian soil, the new country was scarcely viable and the population miserably poor.

While it is true that India owes its independence to anglicized Indians, its economic expansion, agricultural progress and the stability of its institutions attest to the vitality of its democracy. The only threat the country has encountered since its creation is the personality cult surrounding the leaders of the Congress Party, which was in power almost without a break from 1947 until recent times.

Mrs Gandhi

The first of these leaders, Jawaharlal Nehru, prime minister from 1947 until his death in 1964, was the great figure of the new India. In 1966 he was succeeded by his daughter Indira Gandhi (no relation to Mahatma Gandhi), a product of the rich anglicized middle classes of New Delhi. Nine years later, she declared a state of emergency in order to deal with the opposition. Liberated from parliamentary restraints, she combated inflation and revitalized the economy. On the negative side, she also imprisoned her opponents, muzzled the press and courted unpopularity with her programme of enforced sterilization. As a result she lost the 1977 elections, ousted by a coalition. However, it was unable to propose a credible political programme, and Mrs Gandhi was recalled to power in 1980.

Dogged by intercommunal conflicts and rising corruption, she soon found herself confronted by demands for independence from the Sikhs, a minority religious group from the Punjab. In order to put down the insurrection, she ordered an attack on the Golden Temple, their high place of worship. She was assassinated in October 1984 by her Sikh bodyguards.

Her son Rajiv Gandhi replaced her as the leader of the party and then as prime minister. As such, he reversed India's protectionist policies. However, his foreign policy cost him his life. He sent the Indian Army to intervene in Sri Lanka against Tamil secessionists, who later assassinated him during an official visit. Meanwhile, his government had been accused of corruption and the Congress Party discredited.

Coalition

In 1989, the Congress Party, for only the second time in over 40 years, failed to win enough votes to form a government. The opposition took over in the 1990s. The Bharatiya Janata Party (BJP), the nationalist Hindu party, has been in power since 1998, returning at the head of a coalition in elections held in late 1999.

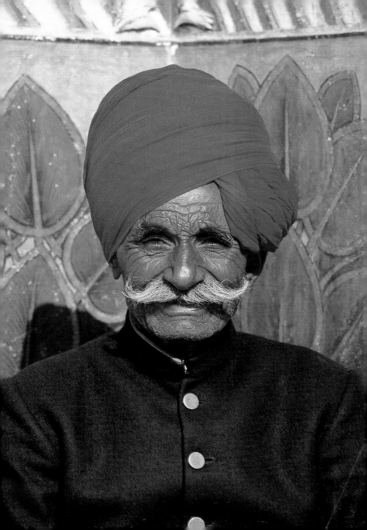

Religions of India

The country has no official religion, but six principal beliefs. The population is composed of 82 per cent Hindu, 12 per cent Muslim, 2.5 per cent Christian, 2 per cent Sikh and less than 1 per cent Buddhist and Jain. Religion is the base of Indian society and the key to understanding the people and their way of life.

Hinduism

For Hindus, the history of the world follows a cycle: the cosmos is born, dies and is reborn. There is no absolute beginning—thus no creator—and no end. Hinduism has no founder and no official clergy. The order of the universe serves as the absolute Truth.

Like every living thing, we all go through a series of rebirth and reincarnation. Our soul, however, is eternal. The final objective is *moksha*, the spiritual salvation that liberates the soul from this perpetual cycle in order to find *nirvana,* union with Brahma. This state, or at least a better life, is reached thanks to our *karma* (the deeds and actions carried out to help the soul to progress); in effect, every good deed results in reincarnation at a higher level in the next cycle. The practice of yoga, which allows control of the body and elevation of the spirit, can also help us improve our karma.

The Hindu Pantheon

Hinduism venerates 33 million gods, who act as counsellors. Of course, no one has ever counted them precisely, but the figure serves to express the infinite nature of the Hindu pantheon. In fact, the number of gods is immaterial, because each represents a different facet of one single divinity. They do not correspond in any way to the Western concept of a divinity. Even their immortality is not innate, because they found it underwater.

The three main gods are Brahma (the Creator), Vishnu (the Preserver) and Shiva (the Destroyer). Brahma, with four heads to represent his all-seeing presence, is reputed to be haughty and a liar. He has only one temple in India; the other two are worshipped throughout the land. Shiva carries a trident and rides on the back of the bull Nandi. He wears a garland of skulls and has snakes writhing round his neck and arms. Four-armed Vishnu

flies around on the back of the eagle Garuda and is the only one of the three to be reincarnated. On his previous visits to earth he appeared in different forms, or avatars: for example as Krishna, Rama and even Buddha. His wife Lakshmi is the goddess of good fortune. Ganesh, the elephant-headed god of prosperity and wisdom, is the most popular; you will see him everywhere with the rat that carries him around.

Castes

Hindu society recognizes four castes: the *Brahmans* (priests and the educated), the *Kshatriyas* (warriors), the *Vaisyas* (trades-men and cultivators) and the *Sudras* (craftsmen, serfs and those of mixed blood). The system is the weak point of Hinduism, as it has led to the unfortunate situation of those who did not fit into any category, the "Untouchables" (whom Gandhi renamed *Harijan*, "children of god"). Originally, society was divided into guilds, but then 3,000 years ago the Brahmans introduced the notion of purity and awarded themselves the highest caste. Henceforth, activities considered to be "pure", for example contact with books, were accorded more importance than "impure" activities—such as shoemaking, which required the handling of dead animal skins. 17

TANTRISM AND THE KAMA SUTRA

The religion of India's primitive tribes included the worship of Shiva. In ancient Hindu texts, the god is represented as a lustful, naked adolescent, a great seducer whose emblem is the lingam, or phallus. God of the procreative force, he is also, in his role as master of yoga, able to commute it into a spiritual strength. Parallel with the cult of Shiva, associated rites, known as Tantric rites, developed throughout the country several thousand years ago. Eroticism and magic predominate; drugs and sexual activity intervene as means to achieve a spiritual state, in the same way as yoga. This state requires the complete loss of the notion of self, denial of the ego and consequently the ideal condition for meditation and uplifting of the soul. Later, orgiastic rites were condemned by puritanical Brahmanism—the forerunner of Hinduism—much as the rites of Dionysus or Bacchus were condemned by Christians. Tantric cults are still practised in India, but are of a secret nature.

The *Kama Sutra* is a literary classic dating back at least two millennia. It is also the most misunderstood product of Indian thought. Because it includes a catalogue of amorous techniques, it has variously been considered as a beginner's handbook or, worse, as a pornographic work. Nothing could be further from the truth. Of its seven chapters, only one treats in detail the different types of sexual union, and all the others discuss the emotional and spiritual dimensions of the male-female relationship. The whole constitutes a distillation of the many commentaries written over centuries by learned men.

The *kama* (love and sensuality) is part of a trilogy which also includes *artha* (the pursuit of economic interests) and *dharma* (behaviour in accordance with religious texts and personal achievement in a moral sense). Its all-embracing aim is to find harmony between these three existential principles *(moksha)*. Given that conjugal love is part of the *kama*, it is only right to carry out one's duty as well as possible, and the *Kama Sutra* helps one to achieve this end. Apart from the 64 amorous techniques, it teaches 64 arts and sciences, including dance, song, poetry, cookery, needlework, chess and dice, chemistry and carpentry. And it also deals with marriage, law—and ethics.

Castes were officially abolished at Independence, but they linger on in many regions, and in rural areas, marriage outside one's caste is still sometimes punishable by death. Women are still expected to bring a dowry, though the practice has been outlawed, and the majority of marriages are still arranged by the parents. In towns, however, the demands of the Untouchables for greater equality are gradually being heard. The president of the Republic, K. R. Narayanan, was the first Untouchable to hold this office.

TIKA AND BINDI

Most Hindus wear a *tika* between their eyes. This is the mark of their membership of the Hindu community. In the markets, you'll see great heaps of red powder *(sindoor)*, sandalwood paste *(vibhuti)* and ash required for its preparation. The resulting mixture may be applied to the forehead by a priest as a sign of blessing, or by Hindus during their prayers. Different shapes of *tika* have different meanings.

Married women wear a *bindi* on their forehead. Originally a simple small red circle, it has become a fashionable accessory of various colours and designs. Stalls sell stick-on *bindi*.

Islam

The second religion of the country, Islam was imposed by Muslim invaders in the 13th century. Today, with more than 80 million followers, India has the second-largest Muslim population in the world after Indonesia. Tensions between the Hindu and Muslim communities—which brought about the creation of Pakistan in 1947 and the massacres that ensued—continue to cause trouble on the subcontinent.

Jainism

At the same time as Buddhism, Jainism developed in India during the 6th century BC as a reaction to Brahmanism—the precursor of Hinduism—and to animal sacrifice. However, its origins go back to a past much more distant than that of Buddhism. The founder Mahavira (the great hero), also known as Jina (the Victor), was born in 599 BC. He was the last of the *tirthankara*, a dynasty of 24 prophets. Like Buddha, he renounced his throne to lead a monastic life.

Jainism is a moralistic religion; some even describe it as atheistic. It does not deny the existence of transcendent beings, but holds that direct intervention of gods or supernatural entities plays no part in the life of mankind. Man achieves perfection through his deeds. At death, he is reborn in

19

another body, and the cycle continues until perfection is attained and he becomes at one with the Absolute.

The theory of *karma* and reincarnation comes from Jainism, as does belief in non-violence. The supreme commandment is to never harm any living creature— the natural consequence is vegetarianism. Pious Jains take the order to extremes: they may be seen wearing white linen masks to prevent any insect from entering their mouths, and picking their way carefully to avoid stepping on an ant.

There are two types of Jain: the *shvetambara* (clothed in white) and the *digambara* (clothed in "space"). In India, it is not unusual to meet Jain pilgrims walking stark naked by the edge of the road. They never use transport, own absolutely nothing, eat only once a day and depend entirely on charity.

Buddhism
Buddha, who took his inspiration from the practices and moral teachings of the Jains (reincarnation, for example), was born in the 5th century BC. He countered the many proscriptions of Brahmanism with simple virtues, such as goodness, charity and non-violence. He recommended the monastic life and renunciation of the world.

This humane doctrine, without mystery, spread rapidly and widely. A political blessing for those princes wishing to escape the power of the Brahman priests, it was largely supported by the noble and intellectual classes. Buddhism was to become a powerful cultural tool and the principal vehicle of Indian colonial expansion in Burma, Indochina, Indonesia, Tibet, Mongolia, China and even Japan. However, within India, it never reached the masses, who were too attached to their own rites and customs. Hinduism integrated the movement and broke its power by adopting Buddha as one of the avatars of Vishnu.

Sikhism
Sikh men are distinguished by their colourful turbans and uncut beards, often restrained by a hairnet. Sikhs make up only 2 per cent of the Indian population, but you frequently meet them in business circles or behind the wheel of a lorry or a taxi.

The Sikh religion, which has no clergy, was founded in the Punjab only at the beginning of the 16th century, by Guru Nanak. He preached the fundamental unity of all religions. The belief which he initiated presents a curious mixture of monotheistic Islam and polytheistic Hinduism. Sikhs believe in reincarnation and respect the rule of the five Ks: they all have long hair *(kesha),* carry a comb *(kanga)* and a sword *(kirpan)* and wear soldier's shorts *(kachha)* and an iron bracelet *(kara).* They venerate the *Adi Granth,* a sacred book housed in the Golden Temple at Amritsar, the holy of holies of their religion. They are organized militarily and claim independence for the Punjab, their region of origin.

Parsiism

Inheritors of the Persian religion of Zoroastrianism, the Parsees came from Iran in the 8th century in order to escape persecution by the Muslims. They are today one of India's most prosperous and Europeanized groups, forming a diverse and strange congregation numbering fewer than 100,000 but controlling a large part of India's economy. Most of them live in or around Mumbai. A community of sun worshippers, they keep a sacred and eternal flame hidden deep in their temples. They do not bury or cremate their dead but expose them naked on the Towers of Silence for the vultures to devour.

Christianity and Judaism

Christianity came to India 500 years ago in the wake of the first ships and still clings on in the south, though it has never really gained a firm hold. The Jews have been in the south of India for more than 2000 years.

SACRED COWS

You see them here, there and everywhere—in towns, in the country-side, in the middle of the road, and even occasionally inside houses. Every cow has an owner, but they help themselves to food from markets and municipal dustbins, regardless.

The sanctity of the cow goes back to ancient times. During periods of famine, the cow was the only animal able to provide infants with a substitute for their mothers' milk. The Indians of the past, by making the cow the "mother of men" and endowing her with quasi-religious significance, ensured the survival of both their children and their "horned mothers". According to Hindu mythology, the cow also assists the dead to cross the river leading to paradise.

Although six cows in ten are unproductive, it would never occur to a Hindu to eat this symbol of universal motherhood. To kill one, furthermore, would inevitably lead to the worst of outlooks for the next life. This is why in some states refuges are provided for sick animals.

21

On the Scene

From the capital to the smallest villages deep within India, this guide will lead you to encounter the peoples who successively occupied the North. The shadow of the British Empire lingers around the monumental buildings of New Delhi; the town of Jaipur will forever resound to the tales of the exploits of the Rajput princes; and Agra is still resplendent with the works of the Moghul emperors. Ancient Hindu culture discreetly hides its erotic temple carvings in the jungle of Madhya Pradesh. Lastly, the great gods of India, unmoved by all the upheavals, watch the Ganges flow past the temples of Varanasi.

DELHI
New Delhi, At the Heart of Political India, Old Delhi

Delhi is the centre of the world's largest democracy. In 1911, the British Indian Empire decided to transfer its capital from Calcutta to this northern province, and to build a gigantic, modern, imperial New Delhi next to the ancient Moghul city. This move was to symbolize the power of what the Prince of Wales could still call in 1931 "a solid Empire, sure and eternal".

Delhi's population is expected to reach 18 million in 2015. The third-largest city of India after Mumbai and Calcutta, it comprises two distinct cities: New Delhi, with all manner of nondescript traffic flowing beneath the flowering trees that border its wide avenues, and Old Delhi, noisy and bustling. Low-budget travellers congregate in the Paharganj district, between the two.

To the Indians, Delhi is their eternal capital, on a par with Varanasi, their holy city. It has nurtured the dreams of all those who have conquered the country, and has lived through seven dynasties. Seven cities preceded it, the oldest of which was built some 3,000 years ago.

Qutb Minar is the proud symbol of Moghul justice and power.

23

In the middle of the 20th century, before partition, Delhi had a strong Muslim population. Nowadays, Hindus are in the majority and Hindi is the dominant language.

New Delhi

Well-ordered, airy and relatively quiet, New Delhi is the least Indian city in the country. You may come across a dromedary ambling along, and a couple of chattering monkeys might swing out of the trees as you pass by. But despite the colourful saris and the crowds of rickshaws, the capital still cultivates a nostalgia for the British era. In the luxuriant gardens of the embassies and the residential areas, turbaned servants still pour tea and whisky for droves of diplomats and businessmen. And the annual prize awarded by the municipality to the best garden recalls the very English affection for herbaceous borders.

Connaught Place

This immense square, named after the uncle of George V, is the lively centre of New Delhi. A humming crowd of tradesmen, businessmen and restaurant owners swarms around what was once a wasteland where wild animals roamed. The major airlines and travel agencies have their offices here and the big hotels are a short walk away. Among them, the Imperial Hotel, framed by palm trees, has lost nothing of the charm which gave it its unique status during the days of the Raj.

Janpath (People's Way), one of the busiest avenues in the capital, starts at Connaught Place, passes by the National Museum and leads to the political centre.

Jantar Mantar

India's first observatory was built in 1724 on the orders of Jai Singh II, the Maharajah of Jaipur, an enthusiastic astronomer. He built four others, the biggest of which

POLLUTION ALERT

Suffering from a chronic traffic problem, Delhi has fallen victim to pollution. A new car is licensed every three minutes! Under the hot sun, the nitrous oxides from the exhaust fumes are transformed into ozone. At low altitude, this is harmful to both man and the environment, causing allergies, asthma and other respiratory problems. India's big cities are particularly subject to smog. But attitudes are slowly changing, and specialists and sections of the press have raised the alarm. Public awareness of the need to clear the atmosphere is gradually making headway throughout the country.

24

is in Jaipur. The various scientific measuring instruments, all salmon pink in colour, are scattered like huge geometrical sculptures around a garden designed for rest and recreation. Panels explain the function of each instrument: some are for calculating eclipses, others to measure time or to chart the stars and planets.

Humayun's Tomb

The tomb of the second ruler of the Moghul dynasty was a blueprint for the Taj Mahal. Whereas the two monuments are of similar design and style, Humayun's Tomb, built in the 16th century, is less impressive and not as white as its famous marble counterpart. The development of architecture in India is associated with the reign of this emperor, and his tomb is one of the earliest examples of Moghul art in the country. Red sandstone cladding replaces the familiar Hindu sculpture and the inlay recalls that of Persian mausoleums.

Humayun's widow was responsible for the construction of this monument to the glory of her dead husband. As the Imperial couple had spent several years in exile in Kabul, the building was commissioned from a Persian architect, hence its style.

Its position in the middle of a garden was a novelty in India. The setting is magnificent. Flocks of parrots and swarms of squirrels have established residence in the branches of the ashok trees, and this peaceful place is as charming as any walk in the countryside.

Purana Qila

North of Humayun's Tomb, the Purana Qila, or Old Fort, rises on the presumed site of the first Delhi. It was built during the first half of the 16th century. The Sher Mandal, a small octagonal tower of red sandstone, served as Humayun's library. Legend has it that it was while descending its staircase that the emperor slipped and lost his life. A mosque completes the architectural ensemble.

Qutb Minar

Constructed around AD 1200 by the first Sultan of Delhi, the Qutb (or Qutab) Minar is a monument whose purpose is essentially unknown. Too high to enable the voice of the muezzin to be heard round about, the minaret was probably designed to symbolize Moghul power. It has been closed to the public since a stampede on the stairs in 1981 caused the death of 40 people.

In the courtyard of the nearby mosque, the 7-m (22-ft) Iron Pillar dates from the 4th century. Made from a metal of exceptional purity, it has not rusted after centuries of monsoon rains. The pillar is said to bring good luck to anyone who can stand with his back to it and encircle it with their arms.

National Museum

One of India's most modern museums, it illustrates the riches of Indian art since prehistory until the Moghul period. Its collection of giant statues, paintings and miniatures was assembled in 1950. (Free entry on Sundays.)

The Heart of Political India

"What beautiful ruins this will make!" declared Clemenceau in 1929, on seeing the huge, almost completed building works of the new British capital of India. No doubt he was thinking of the persistent rumours of independence and rebellion in the air. But today every part of this last great colonial dream is still standing. Rashtrapati Bhavan, former official residence of the viceroys of India, and its imposing red brick buildings still dominate Rajpath, as does India Gate at the other end, scarcely visible through the veil of pollution.

It is said that the plan to transfer the capital of British India to Delhi was the best-kept secret in the country's history and that its announcement in 1911 stupefied the entire subcontinent. Without losing a moment's time, the British drew up plans for the eighth Delhi, which was to be the most beautiful of them all. It is also reported that when the chief architect of the project, Sir Edward Lutyens, arrived from London in 1913, the King of England had already laid the foundation stone of the new city to the north of the old Moghul capital. Visiting the site on the back of an elephant, Lutyens, who was suffering from the heat, declared it poorly chosen. Returning under cover of darkness to dig up the royal stone, he decided to build the future Imperial capital to the south, near Raisina Hill.

The density of trees and greenery which characterizes New Delhi today would have one believe that it was built in the clearings of a great forest. Nothing could be further from the truth. The smallest stone and the tiniest shrub are the fruits of the labour of a workforce which for 20 years toiled on this arid terrain: 30,000 men and women from all over northern India, who were hired to level the land, construct the roads and lay the drains. Apart from the official buildings, 4,000 residences were erected and 10,000 trees planted.

New Delhi was finally inaugurated on February 9, 1931, by the Viceroy, Lord Irwin, amidst parades of elephants and traditional Indian festivities. The party for 5,000 guests lasted for 15 days.

Who could have imagined that only 16 years later the British would leave India forever, leaving behind this monument to pride and optimism?

Rashtrapati Bhavan

The official residence of the President of the Republic is many times bigger than Buckingham Palace, with a façade 192 m (630 ft) long and a surface area of almost 19,000 sq m (204,000 sq ft). During the days of the British Empire, 2,000 servants worked here, 50 of whom were employed solely to chase unwelcome birds from the park. The interior can be visited on request, but only when the president is absent. The palace boasts more than 300 rooms, including the immense teak dining room and the vast Darbar Hall, where the last British Viceroy, Lord Mountbatten, handed over power to the Prime Minister of India, Jawaharlal Nehru.

In the palace courtyard is an unmistakable sandstone column 44 m (144 ft) high and surmounted by a lotus. It is known as the "Jaipur Column" because the Maharajah of Jaipur presented it to the British. It bears witness to the good relations between the princely states of Rajasthan and their successive conquerors.

The gardens surrounding the palace are only accessible in February, or possibly in March. Inspired by the Moghul gardens of Kashmir, they are filled with the sound of fountains and birdsong. Some 150 gardeners are employed to look after them.

Ministries

Still on Raisina Hill, a group of buildings in perfect harmony with the architecture of Rashtrapati Bhavan surround the palace and confer upon it an impressive symmetry. Lutyens, who didn't much care for Hindu or Muslim architecture, chose a neoclassical

1

THE BEST CONFECTIONER Everyone in Delhi knows **Nathu**'s sweet shop. To the east of Connaught Place, in the middle of the Bengali Market, the shop is stocked with mountains of green or pale pink sweets, candied fruits, *gulab jamun* swimming in syrup, and pistachio, carrot or walnut creams heaped up on its counters. A thousand litres (2,100 pints) of milk and 500 kg (1,100 lb) of sugar go into their manufacture every day. The kitchens are worth a look.

Western style. He did, however, add a few Indian elements: the domes of the presidential palace are reminiscent of the Buddhist buildings which Lutyens admired. In fact, he himself described the ensemble as "an Englishman dressed for the climate". The building stone, brought from the Agra region, and the surrounding earth are of the same ochre colour.

GANDHI'S ASSASSINATION

When in Delhi, the Mahatma often stayed with the rich Birlas family, who lived in Tees January Road. Their house is now a museum known as the "Hall of the Nation". Gandhi, affectionately known as "Bapu" (father) by the ordinary people, was not popular with all Hindus. Some reproached him for defending the Untouchables, others for having accepted partition and for supporting the Muslims. Those Muslims not yet expatriated to Pakistan had been persecuted throughout the country since the declaration of Independence. It was on their behalf that Gandhi undertook his last campaign at the end of 1947. Following a lengthy fast designed to stir up public opinion, he was murdered by a Hindu fanatic when he went to pray in the Birlas's garden.

Today these buildings house the Ministry of Foreign Affairs and the Ministry of Finance. Before their façades stand columns representing the British Dominions: Australia, South Africa, Canada and New Zealand. The globes and ships surmounting the columns show the oceans traversed by the British and the countries they conquered.

Sansad Bhavan

The seat of the Indian Parliament, a circular building topped by a dome, lies northeast of the site. Inside are the Rajya Sabha (Council of States) and the Lok Sabha (Chamber of the People). You can attend the debates by making a request at the tourist office or your embassy. The Cathedral of the Redemption is on the left.

India Gate

At the far end of Rajpath, the India Gate is a triumphal arch 42 m (138 ft) high, built to honour the memory of the 90,000 Indian soldiers who fell in Europe during World War I.

Teen Murti House

The sumptuous mansion where Nehru lived is south of Raisina Hill. The house and garden have been converted into a museum. The garden is famous for its roses—Nehru always wore a rose in his buttonhole. Nothing has been altered since the death of the great man in 1964.

Indira Gandhi Museum

Leaving Teen Murti House by Murti Marg you reach Safdarjang Road. Number 1 is Mrs Gandhi's bungalow, but it has nothing of the splendour you might expect of a prime minister's residence. Nevertheless, this was where Nehru's daughter lived, and it was in the adjoining garden that she was assassinated by her bodyguards in October 1984. It is now a museum to her memory.

Old Delhi

Old Delhi, the seventh and penultimate Delhi, is a Moghul city. Its monuments are essentially the work of one man, Shah Jahan, who moved his capital here from Agra in 1648. The "King of the World", often compared to Louis XIV for his extravagance and taste for power, had just completed the famous Taj Mahal. His legacies to Delhi are the Friday Mosque and Lal Qila, the Red Fort. Nowadays, the fort is a lifeless monumental pile. But you'll find something of the sparkle of the old days in the tangle of lanes of the old town, filled with the noise of sputtering engines. There are still many Muslims living here, especially around the mosque. It is magical, disconcerting—in short, very Indian.

Lal Qila

It is difficult to imagine the original fort of the Moghul Empire. What is left standing can give

THE ROYAL ROAD

Rajpath leads from India Gate to Rashtrapati Bhavan along a perfectly designed perspective. From the bedroom of his palace, the Viceroy of India could contemplate the triumphal arch behind which stood (at that time) a white marble statue of George V. Thus, the royal silhouette reminded the king's representative in India at his awakening every morning just who was the boss. The princes and members of the government whose homes also lined this road were equally brought to order by this sight. Conversely, when coming up Rajpath to visit the palace, they had their backs to the king. This gave them enough time to recover their self-confidence and thereby their ability to take decisions.

The statue of George V was removed in 1947, as were the other symbols of British domination. Since then, Rajpath is the scene of the parade marking Republic Day, every January 26.

The Friday Mosque, Jama Masjid, stands on an outcrop of rock southwest of the Red Fort.

only a vague idea, as the British demolished most of the palace apartments and replaced them with barracks.

It took nine years for Shah Jahan to build his fort. The Moghul Empire was at the summit of its power and the architecture of this symmetrical, rectangular building reflects the image of a solidly established monarchy. The white marble walls were inlaid with precious stones, the ceilings gleamed with gold and silver, and carpets covered the courtyards. The royal baths to the left of the palace were supplied with rose-scented water of varying temperatures. Nearby, "monsoon fountains" sprinkled "rain" in the dry season, and a ventilation system cooled the air. The fame of this place spread as far as the courts of Europe.

When the British took Delhi in 1803, they found the Moghul emperor shut away in the depths of his fort, the last bastion of an empire which had endured for nearly three centuries. Fifty-four years later, the Red Fort was to become the setting for scenes from the Indian Mutiny. The massive gates at the western entrance are still pocked with the bullet marks.

You enter the fort by the pink sandstone Lahore Gate, which

30

opens directly into a bazaar which was originally the shopping area for the ladies of the court.

The emperor would hear complaints from his subjects in the Diwan-i-Am, the Hall of Public Audience, where he sat cross-legged on a throne beneath a canopy. At the back of the hall are panels inlaid with birds and flowers.

Private meetings were held by appointment in the Diwan-i-Khas. Here the emperor sat on a splendid solid gold Peacock Throne. Only the marble pedestal remains today; the throne was taken to Iran by the Persian troops of Nadir Shah in 1739 and broken up. The silver ceiling was also removed, but you can still see on the walls the famous couplet: "If there is a paradise on earth, it is this, it is this, it is this!"

The main harem, Rang Mahal (Palace of Colour) has ceiling and walls ornamented with mirror mosaics which twinkle like stars if you strike a match.

Jama Masjid

The Friday Mosque, the biggest in India, was the last indulgence of Shah Jahan. The courtyard can hold 25,000 people, and the striped minarets of white marble and red sandstone measure 40 m (over 130 ft). Stalls and workshops look lost at the foot of the monumental staircases, and the whole area seems overwhelmed by the white marble domes striped with black. Seething with people and animals, the surrounding lanes have lost nothing of their timeless charm, especially seen in the evenings by lamplight.

Chandni Chowk

This is both the main thoroughfare and the heart of Old Delhi, and was once a processional avenue. Starting out just opposite the Red Fort, Chandni Chowk (Silver Street) stretches from a small Jain temple to the east to Fatehpuri Mosque, built in 1650 by one of Shah Jahan's wives, at its western end. Half-way between the two, Sunehri Masjid, the Golden Mosque, recalls some of the city's darkest hours, when in 1739 Nadir Shah climbed onto the roof to watch his troops massacre the district's inhabitants.

There is nothing much left of the merchants' luxurious homes and the expensive shops which gave Chandni Chowk its reputation as the greatest shopping centre in the east. Nevertheless, the famous street and the maze of lanes running from it remain unrivalled for strolling at the end of the day among the thousands of shops, stalls and bazaars of all descriptions selling clothes, jewellery and traditional sweetmeats. 31

JAIPUR

Pink City, The Modern Town, Nahagarh,
Amber, Sanganer, The Road to Agra

The three cities of Jaipur, Delhi and Agra form India's "golden triangle", but whereas Delhi boasts 3,000 years of history, Jaipur is a virtual newcomer, less than 300 years old.

Jai Singh II (1699–1745) was chief of the Rajput Kachhwaha clan, fourth principality of Rajputana, the "land of princes". In the 1720s, he took advantage of good relations with the Moghul ruler to leave his fortress in Amber and found a new capital a few miles away on the plain. Work began in November 1727, and it took seven years to finish most of the construction. For the first time, a Rajput town was designed according to the principles of city planning laid down by ancient Hindu texts on architecture, with nine rectangular plots (symbolizing the nine divisions of the universe) separated by wide avenues intersecting at right angles. In the centre, the palace extended over two plots. The new city was protected by a crenellated rampart 10 km (6 miles) in circumference and fortresses in the surrounding hills.

A distinguished warrior, Jai Singh was also passionately interested in art and astronomy. He preferred peace to war and dreamt of making Jaipur the capital of a unified Rajputana. His ambition was fulfilled, but only much later, when in 1948–49 the 22 Rajput States agreed to become part of a united India and to form one state, Rajasthan. Jaipur became the administrative and economic capital and is now at the head of a region of 343,000 sq km (132,000 sq miles) and 55 million inhabitants. When India achieved independence, the maharajahs still owned essentially all the wealth of this partially desert state, afflicted by poverty. Life expectancy and levels of literacy were among the lowest in India. Despite the enormity of the task, agriculture (which employs 70 per cent of the population) and industry have made great advances and created a considerable improvement in living conditions.

With almost 2 million inhabitants, the modern town of Jaipur has spread well beyond its original boundary, but within the fortifications, the layout of the old town and its buildings is virtually unchanged.

Jantar Mantar, Jai Singh II's monumental observatory.

Pink City

Apart from the noise and the dust, the streets of Jaipur have nothing in common with the streets in other northern cities. They are spacious—as much as 36 m (nearly 120 ft) wide—and the orange and pink-fronted houses are among India's most beautiful. A symbol of welcome, the colour pink was chosen in 1876 for the visit of the future King Edward VII, and ever since the owners have been obliged to conform and to repaint the façades regularly—a degree of uniformity contrary to Indian custom. But Jaipur begs to differ: when the town was founded, Jai Singh offered building permits to numerous merchants and craftsmen, but only on condition that they used designated building materials.

Their descendants occupy the liveliest streets and markets in the city, where pedestrians jostle for space along with auto-rickshaws, camel-drawn carts, cars and vans. Bapu or Nehru Bazaar is devoted mainly to textiles and perfumes, Tripolia Bazaar to carvings, brassware and lacquer bracelets and Chandpol Bazaar to trinkets and souvenirs. Each quarter of the town has its own "guild": near the Palace of the Winds, Johari Bazaar, the main shopping centre, is the jewellers' quarter, which they share with sari sellers.

City Palace

Some of the palace apartments are still occupied by the descendants of the maharajahs, but the rest has been converted into a museum. Jai Singh's successors have left their mark on the majesty of the ensemble, a blend of Moghul and Rajasthani styles. However, some additions date from the beginning of the 20th

---

HAVELI

The town residences of provincial maharajahs or the homes of prosperous merchants, *haveli* are in fact palaces. If their exterior appearance is deliberately modest, the interior courtyards are immense, the walls richly decorated and the storeys numerous and all sumptuously furnished.

Each town in Rajasthan has a few, but many are abandoned, and the antique shops of the region are stuffed with objects from the *haveli*. Old barred window frames abound—you'll have seen them in furniture shops at home, covered with glass and transformed into coffee tables. In Jaipur, the Raj Palace and Samode *haveli* are two examples of these residences which have been converted into luxurious hotels.

century, such as Mubarak Mahal (Palace of Welcome), designed to accommodate important guests. This strange construction looks rather like a huge box inlaid with ivory. It now houses costumes of the old maharajahs, musical instruments, pottery and Moghul crafts. In the other buildings, you can see the arms of Rajput warriors and collection of royal photographs, in addition to the giant silver jars used by Nadho Singh II during a visit to England in 1901 to carry a supply of Ganges water for his personal consumption.

Hawa Mahal

Built in 1799 by Lalchand Usta for the Maharajah Sawaj Pratap Singh, who reigned from 1778 to 1803, the Palace of the Winds is one of Jaipur's great attractions. Situated in the heart of the old city, it is part of the City Palace complex. In very singular style, it is five storeys high, but has a depth of only a few yards. Its pink sandstone façade pierced by numerous latticework windows and decorated by three-sided balconies are an indication of its original function, which was to

---

THE LAST MAHARAJAH

The Rajputs ruled the region for a good thousand years. In 1947, the creation of a democratic India put an end to their power. To encourage them to integrate in a united India, the government offered them various privileges, including an annual pension. But in 1971, Indira Gandhi abolished these privileges and many maharajahs have since been forced to open their palaces to the public in order to pay for the upkeep.

In Jaipur, Rambagh Palace has not escaped this economic necessity. This luxurious residence, now converted into an hotel, was the home of the last Maharajah of Jaipur, Man Singh II, and his third wife Gayatri Devi. The couple had a colossal fortune and an extravagant lifestyle: the roads were closed to traffic an hour before they went out by car, so that there would be no dust in the air and their water was brought every morning from a special spring by four servants and a soldier. The couple ceased to rule over the town in 1947, but lost nothing of their popularity with the locals. In fact, when the Maharani Devi stood for the regional legislative elections against the Congress Party in 1962, she smashed all the records ever obtained by the opposition. Man Singh II died accidentally in England in 1970. His descendants still live in private apartments within the City Palace.

allow the ladies of the royal harem to watch street life and processions while remaining hidden from public view.

The building was designed with natural air conditioning. From the top there is a fine view over Jaipur.

Jantar Mantar

This huge observatory open to the sky (its name means "instruments of magic formulae") was created by Jai Singh II in 1728. The maharajah was fascinated by the movement of the sun, the planets and the stars and built five observatories in all, the one in Delhi being the first ever established in India (1724). Three others were set up at Ujjain, Varanasi and Mathura when he became governor of Agra. The Mathura observatory has been destroyed, and of the remainder, that of Jaipur is the most impressive. Jai Singh kept himself informed of the work of Kepler, Galileo, Cassini and Newton, and made enquiries about the latest European discoveries before equipping the site.

The Jaipur observatory consists of a multitude of measuring instruments of monumental size, resembling a group of abstract scuptures. In reality, these are serious scientific instruments capable of accurately recording the position of the earth and other astronomical phenomena. The giant sundial, with a gnomon 30 m (nearly 100 ft) high, is the world's most accurate: it is graduated in 20-second intervals and the shadow moves at 4 m (13 ft) per hour. Several of the instruments are designed to measure time, others for calculating eclipses or azimuths. The 12 signs of the zodiac are also represented. Astrology has a strong influence on Hindu life, intervening for example, in the choice of a spouse.

THE EMPEROR'S PUPPETS

The shops opposite Hawa Mahal are overflowing with colourful marionettes. More than a thousand people in Jaipur make a living from these figurines, nowadays aimed at the tourist trade. During Moghul rule they were intended for the entertainment of the emperor and the court. The puppet shows were satirical, the puppets representing the ruler or the Rajput princes. Some families still earn a living giving these shows. Their dexterity in operating the marionettes is amazing: at the ends of the strings, belly-dancers undulate, bearded nabobs are transformed into snakes and magicians play with fire. Free shows are organized in the gardens of the Raj Palace, near the Zorawar Singh Gate.

The Modern Town

Outside the ramparts, pierced by eleven gates, the new town stretches to the southwest of the old city. It has good restaurants, cinemas and the railway station.

Beyond the New Gate, Jawaharlal Nehru Marg leads directly to the Ram Niwas Gardens. Designed in the middle of the 19th century, the gardens enclose a zoo specializing in breeding crocodiles, the Museum of Modern Art (Ravindra Rangmanch), and above all the imposing Albert Hall. This houses the collections of the Municipal Museum: Rajasthani costumes, brassware and woodwork on the ground floor; miniatures and portraits of the maharajahs upstairs. Exhibitions illustrate rural life and the popular traditions of Rajasthan.

To the southwest of Ram Niwas, Rambagh Palace, home of the last local maharajah, has been converted into a hotel.

Nahargarh

The Tiger Fort, on a high ridge on the north side of Jaipur, is known for its exceptional setting and the views all around. It is floodlit at night. Jai Singh had the fortress built in 1734 to protect the town, and cannon were fired to announce the time of day to everyone within hearing distance. At the top is a small restaurant which can propose accommodation in one double room.

Amber

The history of the Kachhwaha princes begins in Amber, a colossal fortress 10 km (6 miles) from

THE TWO LIVELIEST TEMPLES The inhabitants of Jaipur come every day to the **Temple of Govinda Deva**, near the City Palace, to participate in the *puja* (prayers and offerings). This sanctuary is dedicated to the blue-skinned god Krishna, eighth avatar of Vishnu. Govinda is the name that Krishna bore when he was a shepherd.

The little **Temple of Ganesh**, near Moti Dungri, is almost as busy, especially on Wednesdays, the day specially devoted to the elephant-headed god. The *puja* take place at fixed times (5.30 a.m., noon, 5.30 p.m. and 10 p.m.), the key moments in the god's day: his awakening, meals and retiring.

The prayers at the end of the afternoon are the most revealing of the fervour of Hindu worship.

Painted with thousands of flowers in pastel shades, the entrance to Amber fortress is dedicated to Ganesh.

the Pink City that was their stronghold for seven centuries. The road leading to it is lined with bougainvillaea. On the way, you'll see Jal Mahal, a palace of Indo-Muslim style standing in the middle of Lake Man Sagar.

The Fortress

From afar, Amber's towers and pavilions, crowning the defensive walls built at the top of vertiginous cliffs, look like a delicately coloured tiered cake coated in honey. Spread across the crest, the 16th-century fortress looms over the plain, its huge outline reflected in the shimmering waters of Lake Maota Sagar. Hundreds

of large grey monkeys clambering around the fortifications only add to the mythical atmosphere.

The history of the Rajput princes who built the fortress is no less mythical, for the Kachhwaha claimed to be descendants of the sun. But the richness of Amber owes more to historical fact than to legend. The first Rajput clan to have collaborated with the Moghul emperors, the rulers of this area saw their wealth and influence increase as the power of the empire grew. Moghul taste thus infiltrated the architecture of Amber.

Built on a huge terrace of white marble, the Diwan-i-Am (Hall of

Public Audience) is the jewel of the palace. The elegance of its columns was more than a match for any of the Moghul forts, to the point that the Emperor Jehangir took offence. To avoid any trouble, the columns were covered with stucco. But the splendour of Amber remained: in the Sukh Niwas (Hall of Pleasures), an ingenious water channel connected to basins filled with roses refreshed and perfumed the air. An elaborate ventilation system dispensed a wafting breeze and, surrounded by latticed marble, the circular terraces overlooking the lake acted as air-conditioned rooms. Everywhere, the polished marble still sparkles with the ancient opulence of the Kachhwahas.

In the Shish Mahal (Palace of Mirrors), for a rupee, someone will light a match, whose flickering flame reflected ad infinitum in the mirrors makes the walls and ceilings worthy of a palace from *The Arabian Nights*.

Jaigarh

Perched on the heights not far from Amber, this imposing fort still looks impregnable. Jai Singh had it built in 1726 above an earlier position, in order to repulse attacks coming from the east. It underwent a number of expansions, as attested by the many encircling walls. From the top of the ramparts, there's a magnificent view over the plain, Jaipur and Jal Mahal.

At the eastern end of the fort, the Jaivan, a cannon 6 m (20 ft) long and weighing 50 tonnes, was cast at the Jaigarh foundry in 1720 on the orders of Jai Singh. Although in all likelihood it is the largest cannon in the world, it has only been fired once, a trial shot which sent a cannonball a distance of 38 km (23 miles).

BLUE POTTERY

Man Singh I, supreme commander of the armies of Emperor Akbar in the 16th century, became an enthusiast of Turco-Persian pottery. He invited many Moghul craftsmen to settle in the region. You can still see their descendants at work, notably in the Kripal Kumbh workshop on Shiva Marg, to the west of the Pink City, or in Sanganer, 10 km (6 miles) away. There is no clay in the Jaipur region; its famous pottery is made from a mixture of earth and gum. It is shaped by hand and fired only once. The Persian motifs and floral ornamentation use turquoise blues obtained from copper sulphate and dark blues from cobalt oxide. Nowadays, some artists have started to introduce a wider range of colours.

Opened to the public in 1983, Jaigarh (which can be reached on foot from Amber) has several points of interest. In the 18th-century cannon foundry, for example, you can see how the barrels were cast and bored, while the armoury has a large collection of swords and other implements used in warfare together with maps charting the greatest battles in India. In the palace, puppet shows are sometimes staged by local inhabitants.

Sanganer

Paper-making and block-printing are the specialities of Sanganer, a town 10 km (6 miles) south of Jaipur. The technique of using carved teak blocks coated in paint to print designs on textiles has been practised here for at least 500 years. Several thousands of craftsmen work together: wood-carvers, printers and manufacturers of dyes, natural and artificial. Every design requires several wood blocks—one for the outline of the pattern, and then one for each colour, making a total of seven for a design of six shades. The printer presses his teak block onto a sponge soaked in paint, then applies it onto the fabric with remarkable precision, square after square.

You'll easily spot the printing shops by the quantities of table-cloths, saris and bedspreads drying outside their doors. Three days of exposure to the sun and rincing in the waters of the river Aman-i-Shah fixes the colours permanently. They should not lose their brilliance, even after washing at 45°C.

The Road to Agra

The scenery between Jaipur and Agra is not particularly interesting, and the shows of performing bears staged along the wayside do nothing to relieve the tedium. However, it is well worth stopping to visit Keoladeao National Park at Bharatpur, 42 km (26 miles) west of Agra, and the town of Fatehpur Sikri, former capital of the Moghul empire.

Keoladeao National Park

The ideal period to explore this bird sanctuary—one of the largest in the world—is from September to February. The park, also known as the Bharatpur Reserve, encloses former marshland which the local maharajah had made into a lake in 1902. He created a hunting reserve where the British viceroys and other officials could indulge in fabulous duck-shooting parties. Today hunting is strictly banned.

Apart from the resident bird-life, hundreds of migratory species can be seen here at the right season. At the end of the monsoon in October you can spot storks, egrets and cormorants, and from January to March a flock of Siberian cranes winters in the park. In the woodland you may see spotted deer and nilghai antelope. Towards noon, sinister pythons—non-venomous but skilled at suffocating their prey—slither out of the foliage to curl up in the sun. You can get around the reserve by boat, cycle-rickshaw or bicycle.

Fatehpur Sikri

In the mid-16th century, the Moghul emperor Akbar fled court gossip to visit a hermit, Selim Christi. This ascetic lived in a cave on a mountain named Sikri, 35 km (22 miles) from Agra. He prophesied that Akbar, who up to then had remained childless despite having 300 wives, would soon have an heir. The prediction came true, and the emperor immediately decided to found there on Mount Sikri the most grandiose capital of the Moghul empire: Fatehpur, the City of Victory. An Englishman, one Ralph Finch wrote in 1585: "Its streets are not so beautiful as the streets of Agra, but the City is bigger and its population very numerous (…). Agra and Fatehpur are both bigger and more populous than London." According to the same source, Akbar had a reserve for snow leopards, tigers, falcons and tame deer.

Abandoned only 15 years after being built because of a lack of water, Fatehpur Sikri became a ghost town. Nothing remains of the hundreds of houses that once covered its slopes, but inside the walls, the red sandstone palaces have withstood the centuries.

Hindus, Muslims and Jesuits lived together at the court. Akbar, passionately interested in religion, developed a new cult called Deen Ilahi, which tried to blend together the principal religious groups. Akbar's desire for syncretism exploded in the architecture, where Indian, Persian and even European influences can be seen side by side. Amidst luxuriant vegetation, wild gardens and red bougainvillaea, one palace follows the next in a jumble of columns, pools, pavilions, domes and airy summerhouses designed for long hot evenings.

The sovereign resided in Jodh Bai Palace. His harem lived around him, and a room with stone latticework allowed the ladies to see without being seen. Near the Diwan-i-Am, an open courtyard, the ground is marked out as a giant chequerboard where Akbar used to play *pachisi*, the national game similar to ludo, using young slaves to represent the pieces. The white marble tomb of the hermit Selim Christi dominates the courtyard of the mosque, southwest of the palace. 41

AGRA

For almost 150 years, Agra was the capital of the Moghul Empire. Its monuments testify to the wealth and splendour of a state which covered a large part of India during the 16th and 17th centuries. The court at Agra inspired the most prodigious stories all across Europe. It was recounted that dishes of rice were garnished with sheets of gold leaf, that twice a year the people were given a gift equivalent to the emperor's weight in silver, and even that the fish in the fountains wore golden nose-rings.

The extravagance of the court was reflected all over the city. The emperors were patrons of the arts, and their lavishness made the fortunes of many a craftsman living outside the fort. The town became an important trading centre, and when the capital was removed to Delhi, some 200 km (125 miles) away, to escape the great heat, the court left behind a rich and famous city, which attracted hordes of travellers even back in the 17th century.

Today, Agra looks like a large provincial town, and it's difficult to believe that the population exceeds a million inhabitants. The peace and quiet is disturbed only by the rickshaw and auto-rickshaw drivers, constantly harassing the tourists.

Like Delhi, Agra has an old town next to the more recent areas known as the Cantonment (a reminder of the British presence), where most of the Western-style hotels are located.

Red Fort

The emperors Akbar, Jehangir and Shah Jahan lived in this stronghold. Akbar had it built by the banks of the Yamuna between 1567 and 1575, on the ruins of a Hindu edifice. The original plain and simple military building was gradually transformed into a magnificent palace, to which each emperor added something typical of the creative genius of his era.

The high red sandstone ramparts are reminiscent of the walls of Delhi's Red Fort, built later by Shah Jahan. However, the architecture of the two constructions illustrates two very different stories. Whereas in the Delhi fort, Islamic symmetry and form evoke the rigorous structure of society under Shah Jahan, the varied styles displayed in Agra's

Agra's Red Fort is an elegant blend of Hindu and Persian styles.

43

architecture are a reflection of the open-mindedness of Akbar. His apartments are of typically pure Hindu design, whereas Jehangir Mahal, built for his son, blends Persian and Indian influences. The central courtyard is adorned with extravagant carved parrots, a favourite element of Hindu decoration and a far cry from the Delhi buildings, where Shah Jahan respected Islamic law to the letter and forbade any representation of living creatures, human or animal.

Although it was erected during the reign of Akbar, the Agra fortress also bears witness to the rigorous style of Shah Jahan. He added the Moti Masjid (Pearl Mosque), unfortunately closed to the public. Furthermore, he had his private apartments decorated with white marble and built the Mussamam Burj (Octagonal Tower), where he was to die after eight years of captivity in 1666, having been overthrown by his son.

Less than two centuries later, the Agra Fort was one of the scenes of the Indian Mutiny. Within the walls, the British garrison resisted for four months while awaiting reinforcements.

Around the Jama Masjid

In this part of town, a few minutes from the fort, the descendants of the first Moghul craftsmen are still at work. As in most of the old towns of northern India, narrow streets lined with shops are home to a host of tradesmen, grouped according to

---

MARBLE INLAY

Grouped in the Nai ki Mandi district, the craftsmen skilled in the art of *pietra dura*—inlaid stone—work in teams under the leadership of the workshop head. The white marble is brought from the Markana quarries in Rajasthan. Semi-precious stones come from all over the world, and the Indian Ocean supplies shells in hues of green and purple. A thin orange-coloured coating is applied to the marble to facilitate the engraving. Once carved, the marble is polished back to its initial whiteness. The semi-precious stones are roughly cut with a bandsaw, then finely chiselled into strips. A hand-powered lathe is used to file them to the required shapes and sizes. The stones are then fitted into the marble like pieces of a jigsaw puzzle, and set with a glue whose composition is kept secret. The time required to make each object is considerable: three months for the lid of a small box; six months for an inlaid tray.

their trade. Spice merchants here, kite-makers, sari sellers or jewellers there; further along are the toolmakers, weavers and wedding specialists. The dhurrie sellers have the monopoly in the Kinari Bazaar on the main street. Around the mosque, cafés offer a limited menu of spicy dishes swimming in oil; customers sip sweet, milky tea far from the madding crowd of tourists.

Northwest of the mosque and on the other side of Hing Ki Mandi Road, the Nai ki Mandi district harbours the tiny shoemakers' shops and the workshops of the marble-inlayers, who ply their trade exactly as they did three centuries ago. In the 1970s, there were still 15,000 of them working in the backyards of the old town. But the trade has fallen on hard times—there are now only just over 8,000.

Jama Masjid

The Friday Mosque, with its striped red and white dome, is squeezed in among the houses in the heart of this old quarter of town. It was built by Shah Jahan in 1648, in honour of his favourite daughter, Jahanara.

Taj Mahal

"An absolutely perfect pearl against a background of azure" was how the artist William Hodges described it in 1876. The Taj Mahal's impressive size, its balanced proportions, its setting in an exquisite garden of perfect symmetry, and its dazzling white marble have made it an exceptional monument. Eleanor Roosevelt, although somewhat weary of visiting Indian monuments, was spellbound when she came to Agra and saw the Taj Mahal. "With the minarets which stand at each corner, its dome and slender spires, it creates an impression of aerial lightness, as if it were floating. Before seeing it, I had no idea of the meaning of perfect proportions. The silence one keeps tells us that this is a beauty which penetrates the soul." In fact, even the crowds of visitors don't disturb the almost solemn atmosphere it creates. The play of light at different times makes it pass from mauve to ivory to pearl grey or gold.

History

The Taj Mahal is a mausoleum. Shah Jahan dedicated it to the memory of his favourite wife, Mumtaz Mahal, who died in 1631 after 17 years of marriage, while giving birth to their 14th child. In his despair, the emperor threw all his energy into creating a monument to express his grief, which would surpass in beauty all the other wonders of the world. The work took 22 years and 20,000 workers.

45

Within the octagonal chamber are the empty tombs of Mumtaz and Shah Jahan. The real tombs are in the basement.

Architecture

Shah Jahan imposed Islamic architecture on India. It is claimed that the architect of the Taj Mahal was inspired by the Omeyyades Mosque in Damascus, the tomb of Tamerlane in Samarkand and the mausoleums of Humayun and Khan Khanan in Delhi. However, he borrowed only the elements that were the most appropriate. For example, he placed secondary buildings and decorative minarets on each side of the Taj Mahal to temper the severity of one single edifice. To preserve the essential symmetry of the whole, he built a counterpart mosque next to the mausoleum, although the new building could never be a holy place as it was incorrectly oriented in relation to Mecca.

The Taj Mahal is the greatest achievement of Moghul architecture. Numerous elements of Hindu inspiration distinguish it from true Muslim architecture inherited from Persia. For instance, Hindus carved their temples from rock and left only a tiny space in the interior. This influence is also shown in the Taj Mahal: its walls are as wide as the spaces between them. Furthermore, the largest of all the interior spaces, the cupola, is closed underneath and is therefore neither accessible nor of any practical

---

A MYSTERIOUS ARCHITECT

The mystery surrounding the identity of the architect of the Taj Mahal has inspired many a legend. It is said that Shah Jahan had the unfortunate man's eyes put out once the mausoleum was finished, so that he could never build anything as beautiful again. Another version recounts that the architect was unable to think up a design capable of expressing the emperor's sorrow, so the emperor had the architect's wife put to death. Overcome by grief, the master builder was finally able to undertake his mission. These stories arise from a real and even more disturbing enigma: no one really knows who drew up the plans of the Taj Mahal. Certain authors name a Venetian called Verronea, though local accounts make no mention of a European. Many names have been suggested over the centuries, but contemporary documents contradict each other and many are simply fake. The hypothesis judged today to be the most probable is that the mysterious architect was none other than the emperor himself.

With perfect symmetry and harmony, the Taj Mahal is a sonnet in stone.

use. The mausoleum, like many other Moghul monuments, is like a huge sculpture.

Life Beyond the Grave

For the Moghuls, a tomb wasn't only designed to preserve the memory of the defunct, but also to act as his or her dwelling. Thus, it was always placed in a garden, which the ruler would have landscaped during his lifetime and where he would hold receptions. After his death, his court and hundreds of servants would continue to surround him.

The tomb of Mumtaz was the centre of a ceremony which went way beyond the norm. Musicians and poets endlessly sang the praises of the deceased. The vastness of the gardens and the size of the guest pavilions tell us that a considerable population must have gravitated around the mausoleum.

Across the Yamuna

A rickshaw ride across the Agra Bridge is delightful, and from the other side of the river there is a lovely view of the Taj Mahal. It is said that Shah Jahan had originally planned to build an identical mausoleum for himself in black marble on this bank of the river, and that a bridge was to have linked the two.

47

Itimad-ud-Daulah

The father of the Persian poetess Nur Jahan, wife of the Emperor Jehangir, rests in a mausoleum on the other side of the Yamuna. Nur Jahan had his tomb built in 1622; it was the first structure in India to incorporate the technique of *pietre dure*, brought from Italy: white marble inlaid with coloured stones. Smaller—and less visited —than the Taj, the tomb is a gem, with beautiful marble latticework letting in the light.

Ram Bagh

Hindus have never had much taste for gardening; indeed there was no such thing as a garden in India until the Moghuls arrived. Ram Bagh, the country's oldest garden, was laid out on the banks of the river by Babar, the first emperor of the Moghul dynasty and an exceptional naturalist. The site has been sadly neglected and is now overgrown.

Akbar's Tomb

Sikandra, a town some 10 km (6 miles) from Agra, is the site of Akbar's Tomb. Built of red sandstone inlaid with white marble, it lies in the middle of a vast park overrun with monkeys. At each corner is a three-storey minaret. Akbar had his mausoleum built during his lifetime but demanded so many modifications that he died before it was finished. With four gates all in different styles, the structure is interesting as it demonstrates Akbar's desire to combine the features he preferred in Muslim, Hindu and Christian architecture.

THE THREE FINEST VIEWS OF THE TAJ

There are not many hills around Agra, and not many viewpoints for taking your photos of the Taj Mahal. The **Red Fort** is the ideal place for a first glimpse. From a distance, the tomb has a particular beauty arising from its size, shape and whiteness.

The architectural details are suddenly revealed from the **gardens** surrounding it: stand in front of it and you will see it mirrored in the pool along an axis of perfect symmetry.

To the east of the mausoleum, a narrow path leads to the edge of the Yamuna. For a few dozen rupees, a small boat will take you to the **opposite bank of the river**. The surroundings are quiet and the view sublime.

ANIMALS ABOUT TOWN

Dromedaries

It isn't unusual to come face to face with a dromedary harnessed to a cart in the cluttered streets of Jaipur or wending its way through Delhi's polluted thoroughfares. With its lacklustre coat and sad eyes, the urban dromedary bears little resemblance to its majestic cousin of the nearby Thar Desert.

The camel fair at Pushkar—less than a half-day by train from Jaipur—takes place every November and is a unique spectacle. Thousands of camels are bought and sold and camel races are organized.

Elephants

Indians have great respect for elephants, admiring them for their strength and vegetarian diet, and also for the wisdom, knowledge and good fortune that they symbolize. Ganesh, the elephant-headed god, is one of the most popular in the Hindu pantheon. His father, the god Shiva, having accidentally cut off Ganesh's head, promised to replace it with that of the first living creature he met: it happened to be a pachyderm. Ganesh serves as a reminder to everyone that beauty of the soul does not depend on physical appearance.

India has some 20,000 elephants, and Hindu art is permeated with images to their glory. The princes of Amber were particularly fond of these gentle giants who carried them around in majesty. Nowadays, some 50 beasts carry tourists to the gates of the fortress. Working on a shift system, they are members of a "trade union" placed under government control. An elephant festival takes place in March in Jaipur.

Monkeys

You'll see two types of monkey in Northern India. The rhesus monkey, with a brown head and bright red bottom, is the most common and known for its aggressivity. The long-tailed langur, with beetling black eyebrows, black ears, face, feet and hands and a grey pelt, is bigger but more gentle. Langurs have occupied the fortress at Amber since the days of the maharajahs, living in total freedom under the guardianship of a state employee. The association which takes care of their food supply brings fruit by rickshaw from Jaipur every morning. When numbers become too large some are transferred to the Sariska game park 120 km (75 miles) away along the Delhi road.

Hanuman, the monkey-god, is one of the heroes of the Hindu epic, the *Ramayana*, and symbolizes loyalty. In Jaipur, dozens of monkeys live around the Hanuman Temple. A priest distributes sacks of bananas every day between 4 and 5 p.m.

49

MADHYA PRADESH
Gwalior, Orchha, Khajuraho

When Kipling chose Madhya Pradesh as the setting for *The Jungle Book*, the state was rich in thick forests and wild beasts of all descriptions. And to a certain extent, it still is.

The wild beasts of the jungle have paid dearly for the passion for hunting shown successively by local princes, the Moghuls and the British. The palace museum, in Gwalior, Jai Vilas, is full of moth-eaten stuffed tigers, the trophies of ancient maharajahs. These big cats would certainly have disappeared from the region if various conservation organizations had not intervened. Project Tiger, launched in 1973 and supported by the Worldwide Fund for Nature (WWF), aims to protect the tiger and its natural habitat. Today, the territory of Madhya Pradesh encompasses more than 25 nature reserves (jungle and savannah), the biggest of which reach about 2,000 sq km (770 sq miles). Only a few harbour tigers and leopards.

For centuries the region was the theatre not only of struggle between man and beast, but of ceaseless conflicts between local rulers and Hindu or Muslim invaders. Many dynasties have come and gone. But unlike other states, northern Madhya Pradesh still retains some very handsome vestiges of Hindu architecture. The conical temples of Gwalior, Orchha and Khajuraho were spared the destructive frenzy which characterized the Muslim invasions.

Gwalior

So many dynasties and so many maharajahs have occupied the throne of Gwalior that the history of its thousand-year-old fortress is an inextricable tangle of characters, intrigues and bloodbaths, in which the leading rôles were played by the Moghuls and the British. The Gwalior fort remains associated with the most tragic events of the Indian Mutiny. It was here that the revolt was finally put down.

Huddled at the foot of the imposing citadel, to the north and northeast, the old town of modest markets and earthen roads enjoys a new-found tranquillity. Lashkar (The Camp), founded in 1809, is the new town. It is spreading inexorably towards the horizon, and its population will soon number a million.

The Jain sculptures, carved directly in the rock face, measure up to 17 m high.

51

Fortress

Overlooking Gwalior from a height of 100 m (330 ft), the citadel occupies the entire hill. Most of its palaces and other buildings were constructed by Man Singh, a prince of the Tomara dynasty, which came to power towards the end of the 14th century. Thanks to its formidable ramparts more than 3 km (2 miles) long, this long remained one of India's most impregnable strongholds. In places, the cliff has been steepened to make it unscaleable, in others it overhangs. However, all this wasn't enough to prevent Man Singh, who ruled from 1486, from being killed 30 years later when the Lodi sovereigns of Delhi laid siege to his citadel.

Jain Sculptures

You reach the gates of the fortress by the south or northwest of the hill. Amazing giant figures carved out of the very rock line the steep path. Sculpted in about 1450 by followers of the Jain religion, they are up to 17 m (56 ft) high. The largest and doubtless the most impressive of the groups of statuary lies to the south, stretching across almost a kilometre (half a mile) of rock wall.

Palace of Man Singh

The grandiose palace of Man Singh (also known as Chit Mandir) has six domed towers. Its construction was started at the end of the 15th century and its rather baroque appearance contrasts starkly with the sobriety of Moghul palaces. The Hindu influence is clear in the coloured ducks, peacocks and elephants which decorate the walls of the first inner courtyard. Such images would be regarded as sacrilegious in a Muslim palace.

Bedrooms follow reception rooms and dressing rooms in a

LEGEND OF GWALIPA

Twelve centuries ago, there was nothing here but a wild and dark hill, with a well guarded by the hermit Gwalipa. A great chief named Suraj Sen, thirsty and tormented by leprosy, lost his way and chanced upon this sinister place, where the hermit offered him water to drink. This water cured his disease, so Suraj founded a new city on the heights and called it Gwalior in honour of the hermit. The dynasty of Suraj Sen reigned for centuries over the sacred hill. The well was enlarged to accommodate the many sick who wished to drink its magic water.

At the place called Surag Kung, a modest stone basin still marks the site of Gwalipa's well.

maze of galleries and corridors, some of which lead underneath the palace and emerge 10 km (6 miles) away. In the prayer room, the niches once framed statuettes of the gods. The public rooms—halls for dancing and music—all have latticed openings pierced high in the walls, to allow the ladies of the court to watch the proceedings without being seen. The lower floors evoke the citadel's more tragic times: under the Moghuls, the room where Man Singh used to keep swings was reserved for hangings and the basements became prisons.

Gujri Mahal

Man Singh had nine wives. His favourite, Mrignayni, the daughter of a milkman, was the only one not from a high caste and the eight others refused to associate with her. So he built a second palace for her alone, the Gujri Mahal. Very damaged, it houses the Archaeological Museum and its collection of Hindu and Jain sculpture.

Other Palaces

Other buildings occupy the middle of the fortress, but none is as well preserved as Man Singh's palace. The Karan Palace stands to the west, while the palaces of the Moghul Emperors Jehangir and Shah Jahan were built near Lake Jauhar Kund.

Sasbahu Temples

Two temples, 1000 years old, stand on the east side of the hill. The king's mother-in-law built a shrine in honour of Vishnu, and his daughter-in-law dedicated hers to Shiva. Hindu in style, the buildings were desecrated by the Muslims, and many of their fine statuettes have lost their arms or face. From the promontory, you can see old Gwalior on your left,

---

THE SUTTEE TRADITION

In 1232, the eight wives of a Rajput prince who died in battle were burnt alive in a basin under Man Singh's Palace. Originally, the practice of *suttee*, collective or individual, was carried out exclusively by the wives of princes. When defeat seemed inevitable, the rajah donned his traditional costume and left to be killed in battle while the ladies of the harem went to the stake in order to avoid falling into the hands of the invaders. Later, wives of all ranks were cremated on the departed husband's funeral pyre, whether they agreed or not. The British put an end to *suttee* in 1829—which hasn't stopped certain extremists from practising it still. The British also outlawed the murder of baby girls at birth.

a military zone straight ahead and the wealthy modern sector to the right. An enormous Sikh temple built in 1954 and faced in white marble stands at the foot of the hill.

Teli Ka Mandir

This temple, 32 m (105 ft) high, was built in the 10th century on the occasion of a royal wedding. It is quite unlike Moghul mausoleums, Persian mosques or buildings of Western influence. Its heavy pyramidal form, thick walls and abundant carvings are characteristic of primitive Indian art. The new wife of the king was originally from South India, and the building copies the style of her homeland, as is clear from the small number of carvings on the outside walls. The temple was a monument with a didactic pur-pose: newly married, the royal couple were shut inside for three days with an instructor to learn the pleasures of love. All over the inside walls, carved reliefs show the young couple dancing, kissing and making love. The last sculpture shows them raising a hand in farewell.

Old Town

A stroll through the streets of old Gwalior will bring you to the 17th-century mosque, the Tomb of Tansen—one of Emperor Akbar's famed musicians—and the mausoleum of Muhammad Gaus, a fine example of Moghul architecture.

Jai Vilas Palace

In the modern town, this palace has been the property of the Scindia family since the days of

---

H.R.H. MADHAVRAO SCINDIA

When he took Gwalior 200 years ago, Mahaji Scindia commanded an army of 100,000 sabres. His descendant, Madhavrao Scindia, last Maharajah of Gwalior, born in 1945, retains the prestige of the title earned in those glorious days. His faithful subjects refer to him as "His Royal Highness", and throngs of secretaries and servants bow when he passes or scatter him with rose petals. The inhabitants of Gwalior actually carried him bodily to take his place in parliament at the age of 26. Since then, this nabob, who campaigns for contraception, for economic expansion and for cricket, has retained his seat. Prime Minister Rajiv Gandhi made him Minister for Tourism, Aviation and Railways. Madhavrao Scindia, however, is far from neglectful of his own business affairs, and has invested his inherited fortune in hotels.

British rule and remains the fief of the last Maharajah of Gwalior. A replica of an Italian *palazzo*, it was built in 1874 and has more than 300 rooms. Certain wings have been turned into a museum, which houses a host of objects belonging to generations of maharajahs. There is a Rolls Royce, and a silver electric train set which used to bring round the liqueurs and cigars after dinner. Durbar Hall, with crystal furniture and approached by a crystal staircase, has two huge chandeliers each measuring 12.5 m (41 ft) in diameter and weighing 3.5 tonnes. They were hung only after the resistance of the ceiling was tested by hauling ten elephants up on ropes.

On the Road to Jhansi

Against a backdrop of craggy hills, green plantations and fields of mustard yellow gradually give way to rocks and a semi-desert landscape. Suddenly on the left, perched on a hill, a group of dazzlingly white Jain temples comes into view. Some 20 km (12 miles) from Jhansi, Datia is famous for its seven-storey palace. It has been abandoned but the pavilions and painted ceilings are well preserved. Right at the top, stone elephants sit in state.

A transit town, Jhansi seems at first no more than a tangle of crowded roads. Without revealing any splendours, the fort provides an interesting panoramic view of the region. Built in 1613 by Maharajah Bir Singh Deo, it was taken by the British, then given to the Scindia family in 1858. A colony of monkeys has invaded the ruins and the old British base. At the foot of the wall, a fresco depicts the battle during which the Rani of Jhansi was killed.

4

THE FOUR FINEST NATIONAL PARKS

The **Bandhavgarh** and **Kanha** reserves, in the centre of Madhya Pradesh, offer the best chance of spotting tiger, as well as a whole range of antelope, bison, monkeys and porcupines. The bears and the leopards only emerge at night. Near to Gwalior or to Khajuraho, the **Madhav** and **Panna** parks also give sanctuary to tigers. The first is a refuge for deer, and crocodiles lie in wait in Lake Sakhya Sagar. The second shelters various wild species.

Orchha

On the road from Jhansi to Khajuraho, the serene village of Orchha is like something out of a fairy tale. The 16-km (10-mile) stretch between Jhansi and Orchha is enchanting. Expanses of water shimmer behind groves of dazzling green, and streams run through the peaceful landscape. The village itself is full of charm, its lanes lined with pink-painted houses, children playing in the streets, and forming a surreal backdrop, countless ruined temples rise up on the horizon, witness to a glorious past.

Indeed, Orchha has known better days. A powerful Rajput capital founded beside the river Betwa in 1531, it became the leading city of the region under the Bundela dynasty (16th–17th centuries). It boasted no less than

---

LEGEND OF ORCHHA

Madhukar, Maharajah of Orchha (1554–92), had six wives. They were all devotees of the cult of Krishna, with the exception of the Maharani Ganesh Kunvar, who worshipped Rama (the god Vishnu, who during his seventh visit to earth took on the appearance of a strong and courageous man). One day this princess refused to go on pilgrimage to the birthplace of Krishna, preferring to visit the birthplace of her own god. The king gave his permission, on condition that she brought Rama back home with her.

Ganesh arrived at the place were Rama was born, a thousand kilometres from Orchha, not far from Varanasi. Coming to a river bank, she sat down and prayed for several months, but the god remained silent. In desperation, she tried three times to throw herself into the river, but each time the current carried her back to the bank. Then she saw, a short distance away, a stone which began to move and to take on the shape of the divinity. The statue agreed to accompany her, but on three conditions: first, the Maharani should walk home carrying the stone god; second, once the statue was set down in Orchha it should never be moved; and third, Rama demanded to be revered as a king.

Hearing of these events, Madhukar hastened to build the temple of Chaturbhuj, where he planned to welcome the god. But Ganesh returned to Orchha before the temple was completed, so she placed Rama in her own palace, which she converted into a temple to comply with his wishes. To this day, the statue has never moved, and two royal guards watch over it as if it were a king.

Behind its rural aspect, Orchha hides an unexpected history and the ruins of numerous temples.

45 temples for more than 70,000 inhabitants. Bir Singh Deo, who built the fortress of Jhansi, came to the throne in 1605. He was defeated in 1627 by the armies of Aurangzeb, only 13 years old at the time. Orchha enjoyed a flourishing 17th century, but in 1783 lost its status as capital to the nearby town of Tikamgadh.

Temples and Palaces

In the village centre, a massive platform supports the Chaturbhuj Temple. King Madhukar, predecessor of Bir Singh Deo, had it built for Ganesh Kunwari with the intention of placing the statue of Rama there. From the top of the steps of the spiral staircase, the temple offers a complete panorama of the surroundings, in particular the city and the other temples. Nearby, Ram Raja glows with over-bright colours—yellow and salmon pink. This old palace is the busiest place of worship in Orchha.

Just west of the village, the temple of Lakshimi Narayan (1662) is a curiosity in itself. Bir Singh Deo had it made of moulded bricks, a building material usually kept for fortresses, and it was renovated by Prithvi Singh in 1793. Ceilings and walls are covered with well-preserved frescoes depicting the fort of 57

Jhansi and animals of all kinds. There are some interesting battle scenes between British and Moghul forces. The military uniforms and life in the camps are shown in precise detail, and the British are shown in caricature, all sporting large curling moustaches.

Cross the Betwa to reach the Raj Mahal, one-time residence of Madhukar. It retains some fine wall paintings. A few hundred vultures live in the towers, and at dawn or dusk you'll probably see one of them setting off on its sinister rounds. The adjacent Sheesh Mahal, once accommodation for the king's guests, is now a hotel. Its upper floors offer an ideal vantage point for admiring the landscape. Below, the Rai Praveen Mahal bears the name of the poetess for whom it was built in 1676. Surrounded by a magnificent garden and equipped with an elaborate water-supply system, it was designed to make life pleasant for Rai Praveen. Further south, the *chhatri*, memorials to the kings of Orchha, lie by the river. Despite their somewhat dilapidated state, they are interesting to see.

PHOOLAN DEVI, BANDIT QUEEN

A political figure who took up the cause of the Untouchables, and a national heroine known in India as the "Bandit Queen", Phoolan Devi is also the quasi-mythical leading character in a film which has enjoyed international success. But between Agra and Gwalior, the Chambal Valley still trembles at the memory of the 55 killings she carried out there. Long before she appeared on television as a neat little woman in an impeccable sari, Phoolan Devi was the leader of the Dacoits, armed bandits who live in the forests of northern Madhya Pradesh and terrorize the local population.

Born into a low caste and married at 11 years of age to a man more than 20 years her senior (in exchange for a cow), raped by police and by wealthy landowners, Phoolan Devi fell into the hands of the Dacoits and under the spell of their desire for vengeance against India's inegalitarian society. She was to become their most fervent and most feared member. Her spectacular arrest before the cameras of Indian television began her notoriety. A sentence of 11 years imprisonment turned her into a living legend.

Since her release from prison, Phoolan Devi has learned to read and write, married and served as a member of the Indian parliament. But threatened by further imprisonment in 1997, she returned into hiding.

Khajuraho

This is one of the best-known sites in the whole of the subcontinent. Its temples and their legendary erotic carvings are one of the most recognizable images of India in the West—no doubt because this artistic celebration of life and its pleasures is so contrary to the values of the Old Testament. The erotic scenes, however, don't occupy more than ten per cent of the temple friezes. Scenes of hunting, work, battle, bathing, feasting, resting—indeed all aspects of life and love are also depicted.

Unlike the *Kama Sutra*—which celebrates "healthy" lovemaking—the temples display rather more daring images. The most astonishing is undoubtedly that of a man "engaged" with a horse, under the horrified gaze of his companions. Such scenes of zoophilia, although rare, are enough to raise questions about the origin and significance of the erotic carvings at Khajuraho. Could they simply be didactic illustrations of the *Kama Sutra*? Or are they images from Tantric philosophy, which holds that sexual relations allow the soul to leave the body and attain the ultimate liberation, or *moksha*?

Mysterious Origins

The site is totally enigmatic. No one knows the origins of the hundreds of craftsmen needed to carry out such a gigantic work. Nor can anyone explain why the carvings escaped the attention of the Muslims. Of the original 85 temples, 25 have survived.

They were built by the Chandela kings in the 9th and 10th centuries. After more than 500 years of power, the Chandela had to surrender to the Moghuls, and their capital Khajuraho sank into obscurity as a remote village. Today, the town has no more than about 8,000 inhabitants.

There are three main groups of temples, eastern, western and southern. Adjacent to modern Khajuraho, the western group, comprising eight temples, is considered the finest; the southern is the least interesting.

The architecture of Khajuraho's monuments was inspired by ancient Hindu texts, according to which temples are a symbol of the indestructible universal order. For this reason, places of worship were given the appearance of monoliths by carving them out of the rock. Somewhere around the beginning of the second millennium, for reasons of convenience, their architects began to build with stone while still remaining faithful to older techniques. The walls were made thick and solid and the empty spaces restricted. From an architectural viewpoint, the Hindu ideal is a sort of mono-

Famous the world over, the erotic sculptures of Khajuraho only represent a small portion of the temple friezes.

lithic tower with a very cramped interior.

The Khajuraho temples all incorporate five essential elements in their design: the porch opens into an ante-room, which in turn opens onto the main hall. From there, a vestibule leads to a shrine sheltering the divinity. Some of the monuments are made of granite but mainly pink, ochre and pale yellow sandstone quarried at Panna was used. The entrances face east.

Western Group

Seven of the eight temples stand among flower beds within a park. Only Matangesvara, still in use, is outside the enclosure. It contains a lingam, the symbol of Shiva, which is $2^1/2$ m ($8^1/2$ ft) high.

Dedicated to Shiva, Kandariya Mahadeva is the biggest shrine at Khajuraho, 31 m (102 ft) high, and the most successful from an architectural and artistic point of view. The erotic scenes of its carved processional friezes are remarkable, with more than 200 statues inside and over 600 outside in three bands: figures of gods, goddesses, musicians and erotic groups. They are among the most explicit in Khajuraho and only slightly more modest than those of the neighbouring Jagadamba temple, which shares the same platform at the back of the park, along with the little Mahadeva temple.

The carvings are of admirable finesse and elegance. Each panel is about a metre (3 ft) long, some temples having up to 800 panels. The king is identified by his beard and by his richly caparisoned horse. Celestial nymphs, dancers and women in general are carved with particular delicacy.

The oldest temple of the group is Lakshmana, dating from about AD 950, richly carved and one of the best-preserved. A procession of elephants, horses, soldiers, acrobats and dancers parades around the basement; gods and goddesses, graceful nymphs, groups of lovers, ecstatic minstrels, battle and hunting scenes cover the sides.

The small Varaha temple contains a gigantic carved boar in highly polished sandstone dating from the early 10th century. He is one of the avatars of Vishnu, to whom the temple is dedicated.

In the northeast corner, a large statue of the bull Nandi, Shiva's mount, opposite the Vishvanatha temple, identifies it as a shrine to Shiva. The sculptures of women here are particularly evocative.

Eastern Group

At the edge of the old village, this group includes three Jain temples. The largest, Parsvanatha, is re- markable for the delicacy of the decoration—note the woman making up her eyes with kohl.

Next to it, Adinatha houses a startling black image, the only Jain element in the building. Shantinatha is a relatively modern shrine containing antique pieces including a statue of Adinatha $4^{1}/_{2}$ m (15 ft) tall.

Within the enclosure is a Jain Museum, a circular gallery displaying the statues of 24 *tirthankara*, the ancient Jain masters.

Old Village

A stroll around old Khajurajo is the best way of soaking up an authentic Hindu atmosphere. The house doorways stand open, permitting glimpses of everyday life inside. Busy streets lead to the heart of the village and its central feature, the well. The entire village congregates in this small square where they come to cool off, wash or fetch water.

Panna

The Panna National Park is about 50 km (30 miles) from Khajuraho. Its dry vegetation, groves and wooded stretches shelter an abundance of wildlife. Nearby there are diamond mines where you can get an idea of the methods of extraction. Along the road to Panna, you'll see the magnificent Raneh Falls, tumbling through luxuriant foliage.

VARANASI
The Banks of the Ganges, Chowk, Two Hindu Temples, Sarnath, Ramnagar

Varanasi, formerly known as Benares, is the holy city of the Hindu religion and its religious and cultural centre. A much frequented place of pilgrimage, it's the city where all Hindus dream of dying, because from here the soul passes more quickly to nirvana.

It is also one of the most ancient cities in the world. But its temples have so often been sacked by invaders and its walls so often destroyed by the angry floods of the Ganges that it is difficult to imagine how once it must have looked. The "eternal city" nevertheless lives up to its reputation: in its labyrinthine streets, and by the immense banks and staircases of the sacred river, the atmosphere is permeated with mysticism and the past is so tangible that Varanasi seems to rise out of the mists of time.

At the heart of an overpopulated rural region, the old town spreads along the western bank of the Ganges. In the interior, the streets lined with tall houses seethe with one and a half million people. They throng the picturesque markets and rattle through the streets in rickshaws; the air swirls with suffocating dust and intoxicating smells, and cows wander everywhere. There is absolutely no comparison with the wide shady avenues of the Cantonment, the modern district of airline offices, large hotels and fashionable restaurants.

You don't visit Varanasi: you see it and breathe it. Most of the temples, such as the Durga and the Bharat Mata, are only of moderate interest, and the finest monuments are closed to the public. That leaves the streets, the *ghats* and the markets.

The Banks of the Ganges

The sacred river where millions of Hindus come each year to purify themselves in the waters is one of the world's dirtiest waterways. The level of pollution in the water at Varanasi is about ten times higher than it should be, a situation partly due to chemical fertilizers and the industries of urban centres, not to mention the thousands of pilgrims who cremate their dead on the riverbank. It isn't at all unusual to see the

The pilgrims at their daily ablutions on the ghats is one of the most fascinating sights of Varanasi.

bloated cadavers of animals or the partially incinerated remains of human bodies floating by, and it takes some time to get used to it. Nevertheless, Hindu ascetics maintain that whoever believes in the purity of the river can bathe and drink its holy water without the slightest risk of infection. In fact, every day thousands of Indians come here to perform their *puja* (prayers and offerings) and their ablutions, providing the most fascinating spectacle the city has to offer.

The Ghats

These huge flights of stairs lining the river bank from one end of town to the other are the principal attraction of Varanasi. Because their foundations are below water level, palaces and conical temples tilt ominously. Every monsoon causes more damage. Some of the *ghats*, such as Tulsidas, have collapsed and others have had to be rebuilt.

Many a maharajah wishing to end his days in the holy city built a palace by the river. As a consequence, most of the *ghats* belong to them. Between Raj Ghat (to the north) and Nagwa Ghat (to the south) there are some 25 staircases of varying width. Notable among them are the Dasaswamedh, central and very busy, and the Manikarnika, where cremations take place.

At dawn the light over the *ghats* is at its most spectacular. From the boats which ply the river, the sight of the *sadhu* praying or bathing is unforgettable.

Sacred Steps

The thousands of steps leading down to the river, where so many Hindu legends have flourished, are rich in holy places. Above Manikarnika Ghat, a pool of the same name is filled, so it is said, with the perspiration of Shiva. The god is traditionally held to have dug the well in order to

THE FIVE GHATS OF THE PILGRIM ROUTE

At the southern extremity of the old city, **Asi Ghat** is the first of five special stairways assigned as baths. In order to accomplish the great sacrament of purification, they must be visited in a prescribed sequence on the same day. After Asi, the pilgrim route proceeds to **Dasaswamedh**, **Barnasangam**, **Panchganga** and, lastly, **Manikarnika Ghat**.

recover the earring which the goddess Parvati dropped in this very place.

At Charandpaduka, between the well and the *ghat*, a slab bears the footprints of Vishnu. The footsteps of another celebrated saint are to be seen on the Dattatreya Ghat. Further along, near Trilochan Ghat, two towers rising from the Ganges mark the point where the water is particularly sacred.

Cremation

This ancestral custom is widespread throughout India and is derived from ancient sacred writings which state that fire helps the soul to reach paradise. Not only is Varanasi the holy city of the Hindus, but it is also the city of death. Hindus from all over India come here to die or to cremate their dead when their financial circumstances permit. It is quite common to see funeral processions in the streets. The body, wrapped in red, white or yellow cloth according to the sex and caste of the deceased, is carried on foot to Manikarnika or Jalsain Ghat. Only the men accompany the corpse to the funeral pyre.

The sight of burning bodies in the night is hallucinatory. The ashes are finally borne away by the Ganges. Unfortunately, wood is becoming increasingly expensive and many families cannot afford to buy enough to consume the whole body. This is why half-burnt corpses are regularly thrown into the river. In Varanasi, one man has the monopoly of wood sales—an Untouchable perhaps, but immensely rich.

Sadhu

The holy city inevitably attracts crowds of *sadhu*. These ascetics have sacrificed everything for their gods and devote themselves

---

THE LEGEND OF THE GANGES

The Ganges is the sacred river of India. For Hindus, it symbolizes the beneficent and impetuous goddess Ganga, who came to earth to purify the ashes of the 60,000 sons of King Sagara. These were incinerated by the flash of anger of the sage Kapila when they tried to steal the divine horse with which he was entrusted. The goddess, however, was not at all keen on the idea of leaving her native Himalayas. She accepted the challenge, but immediately announced that her torrential waters would flood the plains of India. But Shiva caught the torrent in his hair before letting it run slowly to earth. Images of the god catching the Ganges in his hair are widespread throughout the country.

to meditation, living by charity. For Indians, rejection of the world and begging are two of the paths which lead to the absolute.

Although every *sadhu* hopes to reach nirvana, the way of redemption is not the same for all. The two current principal tendencies are illustrated by the followers of Shiva, who paint three horizontal lines on their foreheads, and the followers of Vishnu, with a yellow U daubed between the eyebrows, sometimes with the addition of a red line. In imitation of the gods they worship, they wind their long hair into a topknot. The colour of their garments reflects the degree of renunciation attained, or the specific way of life chosen. Some *sadhu* live naked, the body smeared with ashes. A symbol of death, ashes are considered to be impure, and the holy men who do this are demonstrating their denial of society and their submission to Shiva, the god of destruction and eternal renewal.

Chowk

This is the old quarter of Varanasi, an endless labyrinth of shopping lanes, stalls and cheap restaurants a few steps from the

Millions of Hindus come each year to purify themselves in the sacred waters of the goddess Ganga.

ghats. The only way to explore this area is on foot, so narrow is the space between the houses.

Golden Temple

Varanasi is Shiva's city. The Golden Temple, dedicated to Shiva, lies at the heart of the commercial area of Chowk, half-way between Panchganga Ghat and Gai Ghat. This superb shrine topped with a golden dome was rebuilt opposite its original site after the Moghul Emperor Aurangzeb had it destroyed in order to build a mosque. For the construction of the new temple in 1776, 750 kg (1,650 lb) of gold were required. Hidden behind a high wall, the building is almost invisible from the street, and entry is forbidden to non-Hindus. To see it, you'll have to climb onto the roof of an adjacent house.

Beside the temple, the Well of Kupor, or Well of Knowledge, is one of the most venerated holy places in the country. It is where Shiva's famous lingam was hidden to keep it safe from the invading Muslims.

Mosques of Aurangzeb

The Great Mosque is as inaccessible as the Golden Temple opposite. Built by the Moghul emperor on the ruins of the great temple to Shiva, some traces of which remain, it is a perpetual source of conflict between the Hindu and Muslim communities. Consequently, it is guarded by hundreds of armed soldiers and protected by miles of barbed wire. You can see only the minarets, more than 70 m (230 ft) high.

From the 11th century onwards, Varanasi was pillaged again and again by Muslim invaders. Aurangzeb, completing the destruction, reduced almost all the temples to ruins. At the edge of the Ganges, just above Panchganga Ghat, a second mosque replaced an ancient temple dedicated to Vishnu. It exhibits a curious mixture of Hindu and Muslim architecture.

Two Hindu Temples

The 18th-century Temple of Durga, better known as the Monkey Temple because of the pesky primates living here, is the best known. But like most local shrines it is closed to the public. Footbridges allow you to peep into the courtyard and to admire its red ochre colour and typical North Indian style. Its five spires, symbolizing the elements, merge into one, representing Brahma.

White marble Tulsi Manas Temple, next door, was built in 1964 and commemorates the poet Tulsi Das. It is open for visits.

The Temple of Bharat Mata was inaugurated by Ghandi and dedicated to Mother India. It is open to the public and houses a giant relief map of India carved in marble.

Sarnath

Buddha is said to have preached his first sermon 2,500 years ago at Sarnath, only 10 km (6 miles) from Varanasi. On this sacred site, the Emperor Ashoka, a convert to Buddhism and non-violence after murdering several

---

SHIVA'S LINGAM

Gaunt, with dishevelled hair and coated with ashes, Shiva is the model for his ascetic followers. His extremely rigorous discipline raises him above the other divinities. God of procreative energies, he is a yoga master capable above all of transmuting then into a spiritual force. Because of this power, the lingam, or phallus, is the principal symbol of the worship of Shiva. It is the sign of the absolute. A column with no beginning or end, it represents the cosmic pillar, an axis that holds up the universe. The lingam seen in most of Shiva's temples or on the ghats of Varanasi is a miniature version of this supreme pillar. All over India, the lingam (the male symbol) is depicted inside a yoni (female symbol).

With their foundations beneath water level, the palaces and temples are beginning to lean dangerously.

members of his own family and hundreds of thousands on the battlefield, established a religious centre—very active until the Muslims destroyed it. Of the temples and monasteries of his day, only ruins remain.

The site itself is of limited interest, and only fragments of Ashoka's famous pillar have survived. But the archaeological collection in the museum is worth a visit. The capital of Ashoka's pillar is kept here. Its symbol of four lions back to back has been adopted as the state symbol of India. The pillar, which once stood more than 20 m (65 ft) high, was erected around 250 BC.

Made of polished sandstone, it was surmounted by a sculpted Dharmachakra, the Wheel of Law, which in Buddhist philosophy governs the world.

Ramnagar

Some 20 km (12 miles) from Varanasi, the fort of Ramnagar is still the home of the town's former maharajah. Part of his palace has been converted into a museum, overflowing with luxurious and intriguing objects acquired by generations of maharajahs. Among them you'll see an astrological clock, antique weapons, palanquins of brocade and silver and elephant caparisons.

69

CULTURAL NOTES

Chaupar

This game derives from the same origins as chess, like *pachisi* and *chaturanga*. The name, from the Sanskrit *catus-pada*, means "four-legged". Chaupar (or *caupur*) is played on a cross-shaped board or two pieces of cloth and is very similar to the English game called ludo. The players throw dice to determine the number of moves the pieces can make, travelling all round the board to finish in the middle. It is still played in some villages. Antique sets—boards of embroidered cloth and ivory pieces—are sold at exorbitant prices in antique shops. More recent versions in wood can be found at bric-a-brac stalls.

Cinema

In India the silver screen is the opium of the masses. The country has thousands of cinemas and video halls, and produces more films than anywhere else in the world: an average of 850 each year. Two cities share the spoils: Chennai (formerly Madras) in the south and Mumbai (formerly Bombay), whose gigantic film studios are nicknamed "Bollywood". Indian films, generally cheap melodramas, are aimed at the poorest sections of the population, the middle classes preferring more commercial American films.

The so-called masala movies provide the cocktail most likely to offer the cinema-goers escapism from their daily problems: one half love scenes, a generous splash of singing and dancing and a sprinkling of violence. They last up to $2^1/_2$ hours, and include as many as 18 songs.

Clothing

The long white cotton tunic with matching trousers is rare nowadays. While the young people like to dress in Western style, most men still keep to the simplest of clothing, a *dhoti*: a length of fabric worn around the hips and pulled up between the legs, with a loose, light-coloured shirt on top. You'll see a lot of women in T-shirts and skirts or jeans, but most remain faithful to the sari, about a metre wide and 5 to 9 metres long, draped around the body with one, more elaborately decorated end, the *pallav*, thrown gracefully over the left shoulder (or the right, as in Gujerat). It stays in place miraculously, without any pins or buttons. Beneath it, women wear a *choli*, a short blouse. At one time the way the sari was draped depended on the region and ethnic background. The colour used to be significant, too: white for mourning, red for a wedding, but these customs are disappearing.

Music

Cinema, television and radio pour out endless floods of nondescript songs mingling traditional folk songs and Western pop music. Authentic Indian music, rarely broadcast by the media, is nevertheless alive and well. Transmitted from father to son for at least two millennia, it can be heard at popular gatherings, village festivals and religious gatherings. A marriage of oral tradition and improvisation, it leaves the performer free to add personal touches.

In the south, karnatic music—purely Hindu—has not evolved since its origins. In the north, Muslim influence has resulted in the more spiritual Hindustani Vedic music. It has two basic elements: *tala*, the rhythm, characterized by a number of beats, and *raga*, the melody, in addition to a background drone. There is no harmony, in the Western sense, and each musician chooses his own *tala* and *raga*.

The best known instruments are the *sitar* and the *tabla*. The *raga* is played on the *sitar*, usually made of teak wood and with 20 strings. The *tabla* is a drum of camelskin, beats out the rhythm, while the *baga*, a kind of harmonium, provides the drone. The *sarangui* is a complex stringed instrument played with a bow.

Some instruments have a symbolic significance. The *shehnai* (oboe) is played on festive occasions and the *bankia* or the *dhonsa* (types of trumpet) herald the arrival of an important person—or the imminence of war.

Sport

You have only to see the number of television sets placed in shop windows or in restaurants during international matches to confirm your suspicions that cricket, introduced by the British in the 19th century, is still India's favourite sport. Enthusiasm reaches all layers of society, to the point where one TV channel is devoted exclusively to the game. The passions aroused by certain matches — India versus Pakistan, for example—go well beyond sporting limits. Nevertheless, cricket is the traditionally gentlemanly game, synonymous with fair play.

Hockey has provided India with some of its finest sporting successes. Initiated by British officers at the end of the 19th century, Indians now play this game to perfection: they carried off all the Olympic competitions from 1928 to 1956, scoring 32 goals while losing only three. But Pakistan put an end to their supremacy in 1960 at Melbourne.

Football, developing fast, has not yet reached the level of popularity of cricket. India can not yet enter its team in international competitions.

Shopping

The richness and diversity of crafts in northern India reflect its history and the various cultures which have co-existed in the region. The quality of the work, from woven silks through jewellery to inlaid marble, bear witness to techniques passed down from generation to generation.

Where

A visit to an official state shop or to the Central Cottage Industries on Janpath in Delhi will provide a good overview of the full range of crafts available in this part of India. The prices are fixed and will give you an idea of the cost of items before you embark on a shopping expedition in the bazaars, where you must be prepared to bargain hard. Another possibility is to visit the shopping galleries in the large hotels or in the fashionable parts of town. Prices there are fixed—and high.

Scams and swindles

Varanasi, Jaipur and Agra are crawling with commission merchants and swindlers. Many of the shops claim to be official state shops, but they are not, and touts will surround tourists on the pretext of offering advice. Rickshaw and taxi drivers and official guides are all paid commission for bringing a client into a shop. This can be as much as 20 per cent of the cost of the goods, and you will be footing the bill. The first price asked by a shopkeeper is usually three or four times the real value of the article. If you pay with a credit card, do not let it out of your sight. Make sure the slip is filled out in front of you, not in a back room where they may be imprinting extra slips and forging your signature.

Jewellery

Jaipur is famous for precious and semi-precious stones. You can bargain for the former at Haldion ka Rasta and the latter at Gopalji ka Rasta, near Johari Bazaar. This is where the traditional jewellery, *meenakari*, is produced—combining gold, gemstones and floral designs in enamel. They also make items in classical Indian or European styles. It is better to avoid M.I. Road.

Marble

The walls of the Taj Mahal are decorated with semi-precious

stones, cut, carved and inlaid in white marble. In Nai ki Mandi, the old Muslim quarter of Agra, or in the state companies within the Cantonment, all kinds of objects are manufactured in the same way: tables, ashtrays, chessboards, etc. The time required to produce a piece is considerable—three months for the lid of a small box, six months for a tray—and prices are set accordingly.

Carpets

In Jaipur, the manufacture of wool or silk carpets is a tradition which goes back to the 18th century. Cooperatives such as the Maharajah Art Palace work with the villagers from the surrounding countryside, supplying them with looms and the necessary raw materials. Each family engaged in weaving has its own motif. The colours are obtained from saffron, sugar cane, indigo and iron oxide. The quality and price are fixed by the number of knots: 288 knots per square inch for a cheap wool carpet from Rajasthan, 580 for a Kashmir carpet and up to 1,800 or 2,000 for a silk carpet. Depending on the quality, a carpet can cost anything from 5,000 to 10,000 Rs.

The cotton dhurries woven with geometrical designs in bright colours made from vegetable dyes are a speciality of Agra. You'll find them in the main street of the old Muslim quarter. They cost only a few dozen rupees.

Textiles

India is especially strong in textiles. Silk fabrics are best bought in Varanasi, where they are woven by hand and printed in natural colours using a technique exclusive to the workshops of Madanpura Road. Production is targeted at the manufacture of the sari. The boutiques of Chowk offer an unrivalled choice. Silk is sold by weight, expressed in grams per metre; you should reckon on about 3.50 Rs per gram for a silk of 60 g per metre.

The Jaipur region enjoys another proud tradition—blockprinted tablecloths, napkins, bedspreads and saris. Also in Jaipur, at the Johari Bazaar, cottons and *kadhi* (hand-woven fabrics) in bright colours are sold by the yard.

And more...

Copper items and bronze statuettes are found everywhere, as are miniature paintings reproduced on antique paper. You'll also see attractive engraved and lacquered brassware and blue pottery in Jaipur. Antique shops are overflowing with fine pieces. Stock up on spices in the markets: saffron is good value and the pepper fragrant.

Dining Out

Northern India, unlike the South, is not vegetarian and its specialities are less highly spiced, although curries are the basis of the daily diet. Deliciously aromatic, Indian cookery combines all the exotic flavours of a country rich in spices—cardamom, cloves, ginger, pepper. And for ultimate eating satisfaction, it is perfectly acceptable to eat with your fingers.

Curries

These are India's staple dish. Curry is not a plant nor even the yellow powder on supermarket shelves, but a subtle blend of spices *(masala)*, which includes cumin, coriander and fenugreek, to which are added garlic, a few cloves, a generous pinch of nutmeg, anise, bay leaves and pepper. The slightly bitter turmeric gives a rich yellow colour to Indian curries. It's sometimes called "poor man's saffron", because it has the same golden colour, if not the same flavour, as saffron and is much less costly. Paprika is often used instead of turmeric and gives a dark red colour. Each family has its own recipe for this sauce, which accompanies most vegetables and diced or minced meats. Curry comes, of course, with rice, a mixture of vegetables, yoghurt *(raita)*, chutneys (mango, lime, aubergine, etc.), pickles and various breads *(puri, chapati, roti)*.

Dhal

This is northern India's favourite dish. Nourishing and cheap, it consists of a rather sloppy hot and spicy lentil curry accompanied by plain rice and *chapati*. In restaurants, you can generally eat as much *dhal* as you like. Many Indians eat it every day, and in some villages it's the only food available.

Thali

Although originally a traditional dish of the south, the *thali* is now found all over India. It was inspired by the ancient principles of traditional medicine, and is supposed to supply all the necessary proteins, vitamins and daily dose of garlic and ginger. It comprises various vegetable curries, *dhal* and spices with rice and *chapati*. In the best restaurants, a sweet item is included. The whole lot is served on a honeycombed metal dish, or more simply on a banana leaf.

Tandoori cooking

Highly flavoured *tandoori*-style cooking is very popular. This is again a speciality of the north. The *tandoor* is a clay oven with very hot embers inside. Air circulates through side openings and keeps the fire burning brightly. The high temperature means that chicken, skewers of meat and various cuts, previously marinated in a mixture of flavourings and yoghurt, can be cooked rapidly. Baked in the same oven, *nan* is a kind of flat bread flavoured with garlic, onions or cheese.

Paan

Paan is to India what chewing gum is to the Western world. Although primarily taken after a meal as an aid to digestion, Indians chew it all day long—it is mildly intoxicating and addictive. The *paan* (betel) leaf is wrapped around a mixture of lime ash, betel nut, a powder called *catachu*, and various spices and condiments such as coconut, cardamom, cashew, rose powder and tobacco, even opium. Recipes vary from region to region and according to the paan-wallah who mixes and sells it. Chewing *paan* turns your mouth red and your teeth black. After they've extracted the last drop of juice from their mouthful, people spit out the leftovers—an unappealing habit, which leaves eloquent red blotches all over the streets.

Desserts

Every Indian has a sweet tooth, and there are plenty of syrupy desserts and various intriguing and colourful goodies on street stalls and in shops. Most desserts, such as *gulab jamun* and *barfi*, are based on boiled, thickened milk with different flavourings. Coconut, rose water, pistachio and almond are frequently used. Rice and chick-pea flour form the basis for other desserts; while *gajar ka halwa* is made from grated carrots boiled until translucent in milk and sugar. As for fruit, melons, green coconuts and mangoes are the most delicious.

Drinks

Most Indians never drink alcohol. Their favourite refresher is a glass of *chai*, hot, sweet, spicy, milky tea. Otherwise, *lassi* is a delicious liquid yoghurt, served sweetened or salted, and occasionally in clay pots which are thrown away after use. Soft drinks tend to be very sickly, but there are plenty of good fruit juices sold in cartons. Local beer is not bad at all, but you may as well forget about wine for the duration of your visit, even if it figures on the menu of some grand restaurants. Mineral water is sold in plastic bottles.

The Hard Facts

To help with your travel plans, here are some useful facts about Northern India.

Airports
Indira Gandhi International airport (DEL) is 22 km (15 miles) south of Delhi. It has restaurants and duty-free shops, open 24 hours a day. Travel time to the city is about 45 minutes by bus or taxi.

From Delhi, several flights a week leave for Agra, Khajuraho and Varanasi. It is also possible to fly from Delhi to Jaipur and from Agra to Gwalior. Several airlines operate internal flights, offering a quality service. But take note, flights are often full to capacity.

Climate
The best season for travelling in the North is from October to March. The heat is stifling in spring (35–40°C), and summer is the monsoon season. In autumn and winter, however, the temperature is about 25–30°C during the day and can fall to 8°C at night. Rainfall is rare at this time of the year.

Clothing
Choose clothing appropriate to a hot climate. However, don't forget a sweater and a jacket, because the evenings can be cool and the restaurants air-conditioned. Almost all hotels offer a rapid laundry service, efficient and inexpensive. That being said, you'll find very good value lightweight clothing of Indian or European style almost everywhere. There are also shops specializing in made-to-measure tailoring. Bear in mind that to visit mosques and other Muslim monuments, you should dress modestly.

Currency
The Indian *rupee* (Rs) is divided into 100 *paisas*. Coins are issued in denominations of 5 to 50 paise and 1 to 5 rupees; banknotes from 1 to 500 rupees.

It is impossible to obtain rupees in the West, but no matter what time you arrive in India there'll be an exchange office open at the airport. The best solution is to take US dollars in cash or traveller's cheques, which are easy to change. The large banks also accept European currency. It's advisable to refuse torn notes, as no one will accept them apart from the National Bank.

Credit cards are accepted in the big hotels and restaurants and in most fixed-price shops.

Electricity
The voltage is usually 220 AC. 50 Hz. Plugs have two or three round pins.

Embassies
The embassies are in New Delhi.

British High Commission
Shantipath, Chanakyapuri
New Delhi 110021
Tel: 687 2161; fax 687 2882

Canadian High Commission
PO Box 5207
7/8 Shantipath
Chanakyapuri
New Delhi 110021
Tel. 687 6500; fax 687 6579

US Embassy
Shantipath, Chanakyapuri
New Delhi 11021
Tel. 419 8000; fax 419 0017

Entry Formalities
You need a valid passport and a visa to enter India. Tourist visas are valid for three or six months. They are obtainable from the Indian Embassy in your home country. You have to present a passport valid for at least six months beyond your departure date and pay a fee which varies from year to year.

Passengers over 17 may import into India 200 cigarettes or 50 cigars or 250 g tobacco; 1 bottle of spirits.

Essentials
Basic toiletries (soap, razors, toothbrushes, tampons) are available in Indian and some Western brands. It is always useful to have a first-aid kit with you (with anti-diarrhoea tablets, for example), although Indian chemists stock everything you'll need.

Colour film is on sale everywhere, but the price is high. Take a torch—electricity cuts are frequent—and anti-mosquito cream.

Health
Although no vaccinations are obligatory, doctors highly recommend vaccination against hepatitis A and typhoid fever, and booster shots for tetanus and poliomyelitis. Depending on the length and type of your stay, it may also be wise to be vaccinated against hepatitis B and Japanese encephalitis. As for malaria, in view of the high risk, it is best to follow a preventive treatment and to take reserve supplies with you.

To stay in good health, be careful about what you drink and eat. Above all, never drink water straight from the tap. To make it safe, use purification tablets or boil the water for at least 20 minutes. If you buy bottled mineral 77 water, make sure the top is hermetically sealed; often, labelled bottles are refilled with tap water. Stay clear, too, of ice cubes and ice-cream, and beware of fruit juices diluted with water. Milk is often unpasteurized.

Eat only well-cooked food, and fruit you have peeled yourself.

Holidays and Festivals

These are numerous and usually movable, following the Indian lunar calendar, so it is advisable to enquire about holidays in advance of your trip.

The best-known is Diwali, the Hindu festival of light, which is celebrated in October and November. Republic Day is fixed on January 26 and commemorates the founding of the Republic in 1950. It is marked by a splendid parade along Delhi's Rajpath.

India is a multicultural country and also celebrates Ramadan, Christmas and many other religious or regional festivals.

Languages

There are 15 official languages in India, though more than 1,600 languages are actually spoken, not counting all the different dialects. Hindi has been the national language since Independence, but it is not spoken in the south. English is still often used for administration and in business

and the tourist industry. All educated Indians speak fluent English and many people have at least a basic grasp.

Media

Most national papers are published in Hindi. There are excellent dailies in English, such as the *Times of India* or the *Indian Express*, *The Economic Times* and *The Statesman*. Weeklies include *Frontline* and *India Today*.

Opening Hours

Indians start the working day at about 10 a.m. It is rare for banks, post offices, shops and embassies to open any earlier. The bank's exchange desk closes at 2 p.m., post offices at 4.30 or 5 p.m. However, offices and shops often close much later. Sunday is the official closing day, except in the Muslim districts.

Post

Stamps are on sale in post offices, certain shops and hotels. The service is extremely erratic, and mail may take several weeks to arrive at its destination.

Telephone

There are many telephone agencies in the towns, identifiable by the letters STD for international calls and ISD for the inland service. To make an international phone call, dial 00 and the country code (1 for US and Canada, 44 for UK). The price is indicated on a meter. Most telephone boxes have fax machines.

Time
All India is within the same time zone, GMT +5^1/$_2$. It is thus five and a half hours ahead of Britain in winter and four and a half hours in summer.

Tipping
Indians, all attuned to the habit of *baksheesh*, demand a tip for the slightest service. The custom bears no relation to gratuities in Europe, being more of a way to ensure decent service rather than expressing thanks. The usual rate is 1 or 2 Rs per bag for the hotel porter and about 10 Rs for other hotel services. In the large hotels, it is usual to add 5 or 10 per cent to the bill for the staff. However, you are not expected to leave a tip in restaurants, nor is it necessary to tip taxi drivers. The term *baksheesh* is also used by beggars.

Toilets
In the upper or medium categories of hotel, the facilities correspond to Western standards and toilet paper is available for the client. Elsewhere, you will have to contend with holes in the ground. Many Indians are shocked by the use of toilet paper, finding it unhygienic, preferring to use water. If you find this difficult, then you should carry your own paper, on sale everywhere.

Transport
The distances between Delhi, Jaipur and Agra are short, representing journeys of two to four hours. The train is cheap and the ideal method of travel between these places. Express trains are comfortable, even in second class. Buy your tickets at least a day in advance. There is a train service to Gwalior and to Varanasi. Orchha and Khajuraho can be reached by bus from Jhansi.

Intercity coaches are generally comfortable and air-conditioned, but the journeys are long. You can rent a chauffeur-driven car at hotels and the regional tourist offices; prices are reasonable. Budget and Hertz operate from Delhi and Jaipur. Be aware that Indian roads are a nightmare, especially after dark.

The most practical and inexpensive way of getting around the towns is by auto-rickshaw, a 3-wheeled contraption powered by a motorcycle engine, with seats for two or more passengers behind. They are much faster than taxis as they can nip in and out of the traffic. The cycle rickshaw, with two passenger seats, is still frequently used.

INDEX

GENERAL EDITOR:
  Barbara Ender-Jones
EDITOR:
  Christina Grisewood
ENGLISH ADAPTATION:
  Judith Farr
LAYOUT:
  Luc Malherbe
PHOTO CREDITS:
  Pankaj Shah pp. 1, 6, 17,
    22, 30, 47, 66;
  Paul Kennes pp. 2, 10, 33,
    38, 42, 50, 57, 60, 69;
  Hémisphères/Frilet pp. 4, 15,
    couv. devant;
  Hémisphères/Sassi couv. dos;
  Hémisphères/Gardel p. 63
MAPS:
  Elsner & Schichor,
  JPM Publications

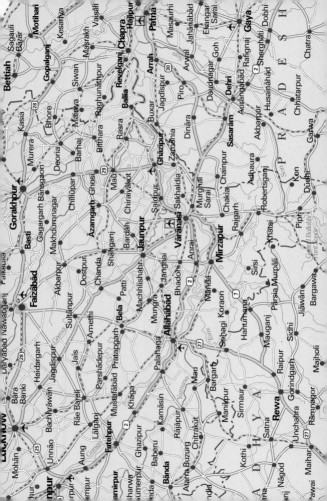

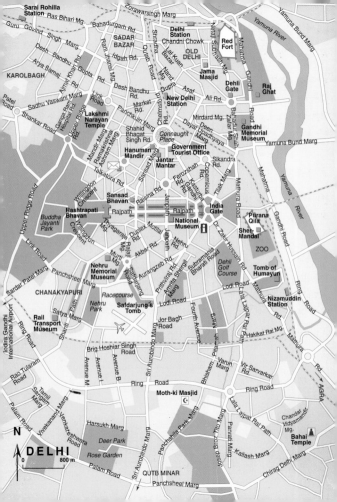

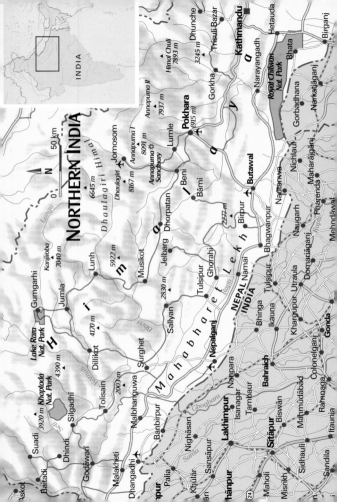

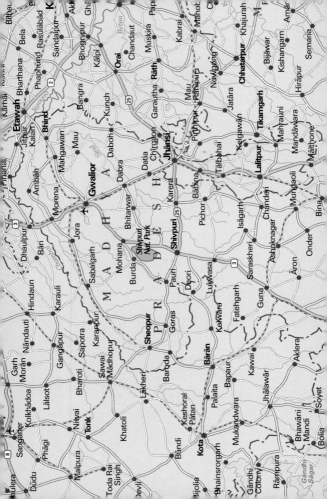

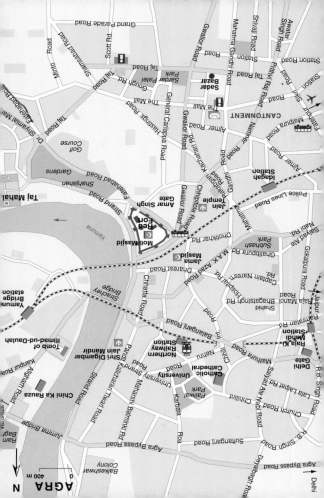

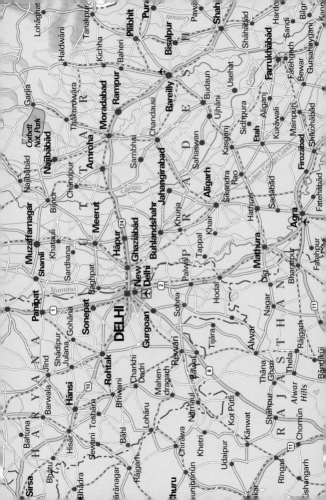